Laptops for the Older and Wiser

BARKING

D1387133

906 000 000 40922

The Third Age Trust

The Third Age Trust is the body which represents all U3As in the UK. The U3A movement is made up of over 700 self-governing groups of older men and women who organise for themselves activities which may be educational, recreational or social in kind. Calling on their own experience and knowledge they demand no qualifications, nor do they offer any. The movement has grown at a remarkable pace and offers opportunities to thousands of people to demonstrate their own worth to one another and to the community. Their interests are astonishingly varied, but the members all value the opportunity to share experiences and learning with like-minded people. The Third Age Trust's endorsement of the Older and Wiser series hints at some of that breadth of interest.

THE THIRD AGE TRUST

THE UNIVERSITY OF THE THIRD AGE

Laptops for the Older and Wiser

Get Up and Running
on your Laptop Computer

Bud E. Smith

A John Wiley and Sons, Ltd., Publication

This edition first published 2010
© 2010 John Wiley & Sons, Ltd

Registered office
John Wiley & Sons Ltd, The Atrium, Southern Gate, Chichester, West Sussex, PO19 8SQ, United Kingdom

For details of our global editorial offices, for customer services and for information about how to apply for permission to reuse the copyright material in this book please see our website at www.wiley.com.

The right of the author to be identified as the author of this work has been asserted in accordance with the Copyright, Designs and Patents Act 1988.

Reprinted June 2010

All rights reserved. No part of this publication may be reproduced, stored in a retrieval system, or transmitted, in any form or by any means, electronic, mechanical, photocopying, recording or otherwise, except as permitted by the UK Copyright, Designs and Patents Act 1988, without the prior permission of the publisher.

Wiley also publishes its books in a variety of electronic formats. Some content that appears in print may not be available in electronic books.

Laptops for the Older and Wiser is an independent publication and has not been authorized, sponsored, or otherwise approved by Apple Inc.

Microsoft Product screenshots are reproduced with permission from Microsoft Corporation.

All prices listed correct at time of going to press. Please check appropriate website for current details.

Designations used by companies to distinguish their products are often claimed as trademarks. All brand names and product names used in this book are trade names, service marks, trademarks or registered trademarks of their respective owners. The publisher is not associated with any product or vendor mentioned in this book. This publication is designed to provide accurate and authoritative information in regard to the subject matter covered. It is sold on the understanding that the publisher is not engaged in rendering professional services. If professional advice or other expert assistance is required, the services of a competent professional should be sought.

Library of Congress Cataloging-in-Publication Data

Smith, Bud E.
   Laptops for the older and wiser : get up and running on your laptop computer / Bud E. Smith.
       p. cm.
   Includes index.
   ISBN 978-0-470-68596-9 (pbk.)
   1. Laptop computers. 2. Computers and older people. I. Title.
     QA76.5.S5737 2010
     004.084'6—dc22

                                                          2010003588

ISBN 978-0-470-68596-9

A catalogue record for this book is available from the British Library.

Set in 11/13 Zapf Humanist 601 BT by Laserwords Private Limited, Chennai, India
Printed in Great Britain by Bell and Bain, Glasgow

Dedication

This book is dedicated to everyone involved in University of the Third Age, an organisation which shows the world every day that the entrepreneurial spirit has no age limit.

LB OF BARKING & DAGENHAM LIBRARIES	
90600000040922	
Bertrams	08/02/2012
AN	£12.99
004.1608	

Contents

Contents

Contents

Acknowledgements

The team at Wiley has been amazing in their support for this book. Tom Dinse accompanied me on a forced march through acres of potential material to help choose just what would make the best book on laptops for our audience. Ellie Scott was amazing in her support, and stepped up to help with editorial and graphics work whenever something looked like it might go off track. Chris Webb, publisher of this book series, got strongly involved to help get the book across the finish line.

About the Author

Bud E. Smith is one of the most experienced ICT authors and trainers around. He started in ICT as a data entry clerk in 1978 and published his first book in 1986. He's worked with Wiley for decades, including writing several leading titles in the *For Dummies series,* and has written several hardware and software buyer's guides. Along the way, he's also worked as a project manager and marketing manager for leading technology companies such as Apple and Microsoft, as well as for HSBC in their London headquarters.

Publisher's Acknowledgements

Some of the people who helped bring this book to market include the following:

Editorial and Production
VP Consumer and Technology Publishing Director: Michelle Leete
Associate Director – Book Content Management: Martin Tribe
Associate Publisher: Chris Webb
Assistant Editor: Colleen Goldring
Publishing Assistant: Ellie Scott
Project Editor: Juliet Booker
Development Editor: Tom Dinse
Copy Editor/Proof Reader: Grace Fairley

Marketing
Senior Marketing Manager: Louise Breinholt
Marketing Executive: Chloe Tunnicliffe

Composition Services
Compositor: Laserwords Private Limited
Indexer: Laserwords Private Limited

With thanks to U3A member, Mrs Gillian Brown, for naming our Older and Wiser owl "Steady Stanley". This was the winning entry from the U3A News competition held in October 2009.

Icons used in this book

Throughout this book, we've used icons to help focus your attention on certain information. This is what they mean:

Equipment needed — Lets you know in advance the equipment you will need to hand as you progress through the chapter.

Skills needed — Placed at the beginning to help identify the skills you'll need for the chapter ahead.

Tip — Tips and suggestions to help make life easier.

Note — Take note of these little extras to avoid confusion.

Warning — Read carefully; a few things could go wrong at this point.

Try It — Go on, enjoy yourself; you won't break it.

Trivia — A little bit of fun to bring a smile to your face.

Summary — A short recap at the end of each chapter.

Brain Training — Test what you've learned from the chapter.

PRACTICE MAKES
PERFECT

To build upon the lessons learnt in this book, visit www.pcwisdom.co.uk

- More training tutorials

- Links to resources

- Advice through frequently asked questions

- Social networking tips

- Videos and podcasts from the author

- Author blogs

Introduction

How this book is structured

This book is written for the many people who want easy to understand and up-to-date information on buying and using a laptop. It uses plain language and acronyms and jargon, such as RAM, gigabytes and MP3, but only where it is needed to help you be successful.

The content of this book is directed in the first instance at PC users working with Windows Vista or Windows 7 operating systems. I also mention the Mac to a lesser extent and briefly mention less popular alternatives such as Linux.

This book is broken up into 12 chapters that take you through the steps of buying a laptop and learning how to use it. I will show you how to confidently choose a laptop that will suit your needs from the ever-widening array of choices available. This book is also suitable for those who already have made the first step of buying a laptop, but now want to learn how to use it.

I will help you get up and running online and show you how to start putting your laptop to use while ensuring you protect your personal details. I'll help you overcome any problems you might encounter, but more importantly, I'll discuss how to avoid having problems in the first place.

Throughout the book you will notice an array of icons including skills and equipment needed (at the beginning of each chapter), try it, warning, note it, trivia and tip. These are aimed to offer helpful tips and tricks whilst you read through the book. At the end of each chapter you will also notice that there is a summary and brain training section. These are there to provide you with a helpful overview of the topics covered in the chapter and to test your knowledge. It doesn't matter if you get the questions wrong; it's just a bit of light-hearted fun intended to help you remember what you've learnt along the way.

Guardian angels

You may recognise the guardian angel from other Older and Wiser titles, and could be familiar with the concept. However, for those who don't know, a guardian angel in an *Older and Wiser* series book is someone who could be a friend, family member or neighbour who has a bit of computing experience. You can ask your guardian angel for advice, reassurance or guidance whilst you are becoming more familiar with computers. It can be anyone who knows a fair bit about computing; not necessarily an expert, but someone who you can ask if you have the odd query every so often. They usually don't mind imparting their computing knowledge when you ask – but if you have a slightly more complex question it might be a good idea to offer them a cup of tea and a biscuit in return for their computing wisdom.

Keeping your eyes on the prize

Computers used to be very large and were only found at work or in universities. A few brave souls bought the first mass-produced home computers about thirty years ago. Since then, about a billion people have bought a desktop or laptop, many of them for home use.

Anyone who first started using computers during this boom in sales, when computers were more expensive and less powerful, often had to learn a bewildering array of acronyms and jargon to spend their money wisely and get the best computer they could afford. But for most people, the need to learn a lot of technical terms is no longer present.

Computer vendors may still use a few incomprehensible terms, but you can just refer to them as a tick list to make sure you're getting what you're paying for. You can put your main focus on getting a laptop that's comfortable for you to use and one that will perform the tasks you want.

Taking it with you wherever you go

One of the most important aspects of a laptop is its portability. This means that a laptop can be 'yours' in a way that a desktop computer cannot. You can use a laptop outside the home and take it with you when you travel. You can almost always use the same laptop, at home or away.

 If you take your laptop abroad, check that you have the right adaptor to avoid disappointment.

The reason laptops are so popular – and so widely used – is because previously having a computer that was portable used to be difficult and often involved many compromises. You needed a fairly big box to contain a fully-powered computer, and they cost more because they used specialised parts. So in the past having a laptop often meant you had to compromise. Paying extra for a less powerful computer meant laptops were not as popular as desktop computers.

I was lucky enough to be working at Apple Computer when the very first Mac laptop came out, in the early 1990s. Apple is famous for not compromising, so their first laptop was powerful, but big and heavy as well. I was late for a flight and suffered, trying to run through the airport with my Mac 'portable', but the components of a computer have become smaller and cheaper since then. The picture below shows the first Mac Portable. You can see that the laptops on offer today are much smaller.

Laptops have also become less expensive, more powerful and more popular. As this book is going to press, a new wave of laptops based around brand new, even cheaper components are appearing. The small, thin laptops that used to cost thousands of lbs, and which were reserved for executives and nerds who loved computers, are now available to anyone for a price around £300 to £400.

Today you can buy and use a laptop without compromising much. You can have a laptop with a medium-sized widescreen and full-sized keyboard that only weighs about five lbs. (This weight is usually considered the dividing line between computers that are fairly easy to carry – five lbs or under – and ones that feel a bit heavy to most people, six lbs or more.)

Wikipedia® is a registered trademark of the Wikimedia Foundation, Inc., a non-profit organisation

Figure 1.1

Keeping in touch with friends, family and colleagues

The first personal computers didn't have any communications capabilities at all. They were used in 'standalone mode', as it was called. If you wanted to share information between two or more computers, you saved a file to a 'floppy disk' about five square inches, removed the 'floppy', as it was called, and carried it to another computer.

Now computers are connected to the Internet a good part of the time. There's usually a constant connection to the Internet when a computer is used at home or in the office.

However, when you're on the move, you can be restricted in just how connected you can be. Laptops are usually connected to the Internet by a wireless connection, even in the home. There are a lot of buzzwords around regarding the different types of connections available; I'll explain a few of them in later chapters. But you don't usually need to know them; you just need to ask how to get or use a wireless Internet connection and people will know what you're talking about.

When you're connected to the Internet you can access the Web, get email, exchange instant messages and even make low-cost phone calls using a headset. Social Networking is currently growing in popularity and it enables you to keep in touch with people online. To learn more about Social Networking take a look at Sean McManus's book, *Social Networking for the Older and Wiser* (ISBN 9780470686409). Staying connected whilst on the move is important to a lot of laptop users so I will explore this in considerable detail later in the book.

Shopping, booking travel and learning online

Almost everything you can do in the real world, you can now do online as well. Some people even find it faster and more convenient online. In other cases you can learn things online that then make things easier, faster and less expensive in the real world.

For instance, let's say you want to buy a digital camera for holiday photos. If you just walk into a camera shop you're a bit like a lamb strolling into a sheep-shearing barn; you may leave without your fleece! But if you research online first you can find helpful reviews from magazines, comments from other customers and more.

You might even buy your camera online, being careful to choose a reputable site. Or you might decide to buy online, but pick the camera up from a store. Finally, you might simply do what so many people do today: you still make the purchase in a store, but you go there armed with your new-found, online knowledge. It doesn't matter too much; by shopping online first you're better-informed and far more likely to make a purchase you'll be happy with.

Booking travel online is another great idea, but can take a bit of getting used to. This would be a good time to ask your guardian angel to help you. It's nice to have someone's advice the first time you book a holiday online, even if it is only to reassure you that you are completing the process correctly.

Part of the appeal of a laptop is that you can do all your online research and shopping, take notes and more, all in one place and at a time that's convenient for you.

Taking care of finances and banking

Initially, when companies began creating web sites, many people believed that the last thing anyone would do online is something as personal and important as banking.

However, once you learn how to you use online banking and other financial services, the power and convenience of doing so will no doubt become part of your normal life. The flexibility afforded by a laptop, including the comfort level of using your very own computer even if you're out of the house or travelling, will be an important part of the overall experience for you.

When logging into important sites online, such as viewing your bank balance, make sure that you are using a secure network and a secure site. It's quite easy to check whether or not a site is secure; take a look at the address line in your web browser. If the site is secure, you will see that the http:// at the beginning of the address becomes https://. Commonly, you will also see a padlock symbol appear in the bottom right corner of the screen.

Challenging old beliefs

Owning a laptop provides a lot of opportunities. Not only can you stay connected whilst you are travelling, but they take up considerably less space in the home and you can take them with you when you go out and about. Whether it is because you want to stay connected whilst on the move or merely because you want to show a slideshow of your grandchildren to friends when you go to a dinner party. Having a laptop isn't all about staying connected online. You can do as much or as little on the Internet as you would like to. There are many other uses for your laptop and I explain several of them as we go through the book.

Here I'll list and discuss some of the negative opinions that might otherwise hold you back. I'll show you where things have moved on, and where there's still some lingering grounds for concern; concerns that are worth paying attention to, but not a reason to avoid the whole topic entirely.

Laptops are for young people

Laptops are indeed for young people. They make perfect sense for students and young office workers who need to bring work home with them or travel on business. For these people laptops are a wonderful tool. What's changed is that laptops are no longer *only* for young people. Laptops are just another type of computer, and computers are for everyone. In fact, laptop sales recently caught up with desktop system sales. For consumers buying a computer for personal use, a laptop is rapidly becoming the preferred choice for all age groups and income levels.

Laptops have no obvious gender bias either. Individual models, even colours and styling choices, might be more suited to one gender than the other, but at the end of the day there's a laptop to suit just about anyone.

Laptops are too expensive

For a long time laptops were indeed more expensive than desktop computers, sometimes twice as much for a typical laptop machine. Even though the price was twice as high, the typical laptop was still less powerful than a desktop.

In fact, it's only very recently that the sort of laptop one would ideally want i.e. thin, light, with similar specifications to a mid-range desktop computer, has become competitive in price with a desktop.

You may still find that a truly bargain desktop computer may have a bigger screen, a larger, more comfortable keyboard, more memory, a bigger hard disk and more connectors than a similarly priced laptop. The point is that these extras sound good, but are probably not something you really need when offset against the convenience and simplicity of a laptop.

What's changed is that a laptop that really can do everything that most people need is now available for a fairly low price that's comparable to a moderately powerful desktop machine. Desktops have advantages at the extremes of very low cost and very high capability, but that's not where most people need to be today.

There's also a subtle cost advantage for laptops that desktop machines can't match. Because laptops are so well integrated, there are fewer separate parts, simplifying the task of buying, owning and maintaining it. So while there are circumstances where a laptop costs more for the same technical specifications, the practical difference is negligible for many people. The advantages of a laptop are available without your having to break the bank.

Laptops are only good if you're on the move

When laptops cost more and did less, except for being portable, you really had to value portability to make it worth the extra price. As laptops have become more common, however, the flexibility and space savings they offer are increasingly seen as necessities.

Laptops are now so highly valued that many people buy one even when a desktop would do. There's even a name for this kind of laptop: a 'desktop replacement'. The space savings and portability of a laptop are valued even in what would otherwise be a desktop setting. A desktop computer is seen as less valuable even if the need to move it only comes up as an occasional or potential requirement.

Holidays are a great example. Some people only move their laptops once a year, when they go on holiday and settle for a few weeks away from home. On this kind of extended trip it's great to bring your laptop with you, set it up and keep it secure in your home away from home.

For this kind of use, you're only moving the computer once a year. Therefore, being able to easily make that move just once a year may be enough to make the laptop a better choice for you.

Challenging fears

Old beliefs are at least logical, and can be answered easily by facts. In fact, most of the set beliefs listed above were true in the past. It's the onward march of technology, and the steady lowering of prices, that have largely resolved them.

Fears, however, are more personal and harder to get at. Typically, the best antidote is often simply seeing a lot of other people doing the very thing causing the anxiety.

Luckily, with laptops becoming so very popular, the fear level automatically drops; if all those other people can find a laptop easy and useful, you can too!

However, let me take a moment to help dispel the most common fears that I've heard over my years of using and recommending laptops. That way you can look at them head-on and decide, in the cold light of day, if it's time to move beyond your fears and make your decision based solely on your needs and wants.

I'll break it

Breaking a computer is a bigger fear among people who are inexperienced with them, even though many people with computer experience actually have broken a computer in one way or another. It's just part of life, like stubbing your toe, or losing your watch. It's entirely possible to break a laptop. However, it's also pretty rare. I've used both laptops and mobile phones for the same amount of time, about 15 years. I've broken two mobile phones and have never broken a laptop, despite being fairly careless with both.

I did spill Coke in the keyboard of a laptop once, and while it didn't get to the circuit board – which would have 'fried' the laptop and ruined it – it was slightly troublesome until I unplugged the computer from the wall, pried some of the keys off and cleaned around them to unstick them. The keys went back on pretty well.

So you can indeed break your laptop. You just need to be careful with it. Keep drinks away from the keyboard to avoid unfortunate spills, just like you would with any piece of electrical equipment. I personally think it's not worth losing out on the advantages of a laptop just because you're worried about breaking it.

I'll lose it or have it stolen

The very convenience of laptops makes it easy to carry it with you so often that forgetting it, or leaving it where a thief can grab it, becomes all too easy. Losing your laptop can be a big worry.

Laptops today are so portable, resilient and, yes, cheap that they're often kept in travel bags with other 'stuff' rather than in separate laptop bags. In my experience this actually renders them less vulnerable to theft and loss. A dedicated laptop bag can be more noticeable to a potential thief. However, as long as you keep your laptop close to you and don't leave it unattended you will hopefully avoid losing it or having it stolen.

Having a laptop lost or stolen isn't really a reason not to buy one. It's more a reason not to take it with you on some occasions where you might otherwise like to, but where the risk of loss or theft is particularly high.

I'll suffer from identity theft and lost data

You can deal with the loss or theft of the laptop itself by insuring it, or by owning one that's cheap enough that you can afford to replace it. Because your laptop has your information on it, identity theft or the loss of personal data can be a worry, but as long as you take precautionary steps this is easy to avoid.

You can suffer identity theft and lost data by having your laptop lost or stolen or while it's still in your possession, by people signing onto your computer when you're not looking or electronically accessing it via an online connection. These are real concerns that shouldn't stop you from buying and using a laptop but do constitute good reasons to be careful.

In later chapters I'll tell you how to manage use of your laptop to protect you from identity theft and lost data. As with many other problems, an ounce of prevention is worth a lb of cure.

Now that I have hopefully allayed some common fears and concerns, let's help you get up and running on your laptop . . .

PART I
Getting your laptop

It's <u>so</u> light and portable!

©2009 Stephen Long

Choosing the right laptop for you

Equipment needed: None needed, though having the opportunity to see laptops of different sizes, and to try a Windows PC and a Mac in turn, can be valuable.

Skills needed: Willingness to learn as you consider different possibilities, then narrow your choices.

Buying books like this one often treat the process as if the reader was not only buying a machine, but as if the reader were a machine themselves. Figure out what you want; gather some facts; process them; the right answer emerges.

In reality, of course, we do things for a lot of reasons, not all of which are easy to write down in a checklist. Emotional factors vie with objective concerns. 'This computer's faster'; 'That salesperson was nicer'; 'This is the best deal'; 'I don't feel comfortable buying online yet'. In this chapter I'm going to go through the various laptop options available to you to try and help you make an informed decision about choosing the right laptop. If you have already bought your laptop, not to worry; read on into the next chapter to help you get your laptop set up.

Choosing the computer size

As laptops have evolved, the term has broadened. It now includes a few subtypes of laptops that give you more choice – but that can be confusing as well.

- **Netbooks**. Netbooks were originally very small, very light, very affordable machines that did less than a traditional laptop. The original 'true' netbooks had screens from 7 to 10 inches in size, weighed around 2 lbs and were neither Windows nor Mac machines. Now 'netbook' often just means a small (screen up to 13 inches), light (3 or 4 lbs), inexpensive Windows laptop. If you're looking at a netbook, be sure it really does everything you want it to do; don't just jump at a low price.

- **Laptop**. A typical laptop has a 13 to 15-inch screen and weighs about 5 lbs. It can be a Windows or Mac computer. This kind of mid-range laptop has recently become thinner, lighter, and less expensive due to advances in engineering. So you can get a good price on a name-brand machine if you shop carefully.

- **Desktop replacement**. This is a full-featured laptop with a screen up to 17 inches in size and typically weighing a hefty 7 lbs. A desktop replacement machine should do everything a desktop machine can do. It's not as portable as a mid-size laptop, but the best of them are very easy to use, even for long work sessions.

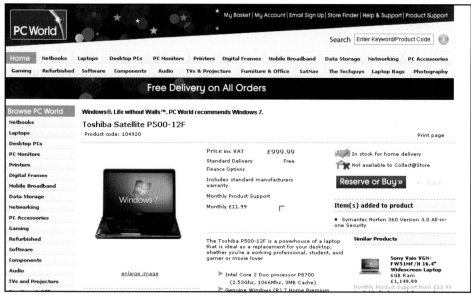

Reproduced by permission of © DSG Retail International plc

Figure 2.1

Larger notebooks need larger batteries – and have room for them. Pay close attention to battery life, of course, but don't let this become the overriding issue on which your choice of laptop is based.

Laptops tend not to last as long as desktop machines, partly because they're 'all in one' – so if the screen wears out, for instance, you typically need a whole new machine. You should also check whether your laptop is covered by your homeowner's insurance 'as is' or if there's an extra cost.

Where to get advice

In the movie 'It's a Wonderful Life', the main character, played by Jimmy Stewart, is about to jump off a bridge, when he discovers he has a guardian angel named Clarence. You may find your own guardian angel when you're about to take the plunge and buy a laptop.

Your guardian angel is a friend or family member who takes an interest when you mention that you're looking for a laptop. Ideally, your guardian angel shops with you – online or in person – gives you advice from their own experience, and offers to help you get started with getting online and using the machine when you bring the laptop home.

You must buy a computer you like, that looks and feels right to you. This is where having a guardian angel along when you're shopping is so great; they can tailor their advice to your likes and dislikes so you get the best result overall.

You should also consider reviews that you find in print and online. Stores and online sources use a plethora of slightly different models to make it harder for you to comparison shop on price and to find reviews that alert you to important issues.

Some popular models do have reviews though. It's a good idea to look at these reviews to help you make an informed decision when purchasing your first laptop.

Salespeople in computer shops are also a good source of advice when they take the time to find out what you want and tailor their advice to fit. A salesperson's advice is better as a resource when you've used online and printed reviews and sought advice from friends and family beforehand.

Choosing the type of computer

A lively choice – Mac vs. PC

For some of us, choosing between a Mac (sometimes referred to as a Macintosh or an Apple Mac – they mean the same thing) or the more commonly found Windows-based PCs can take some thought. It is all down to personal preference and what you want to use your computer for. Sometimes you can be influenced by what your friends and family have. If you have a similar computer to them, it can sometimes be easier to describe a problem you have encountered. If you have the same type you can try their software, try their add-on devices, get tips and tricks and generally do a lot more, more cheaply and easily.

The second most important point is what you feel comfortable with. (And you thought that what you wanted was first! You'll find that buying and using a computer has a big social element.)

If these two elements – the people around you and your own comfort level – both point in the same direction, it's an easy choice. This usually means a Windows machine.

This may leave you wondering why anyone bothers to buy a Mac, as they're in the minority. You may also have a Mac fan or two among your friends and family, and find it difficult to evaluate their advice vs. the ease of going with the Windows mainstream.

If most of the people around you, who might help you with your computer or want to use your computer occasionally, use Windows-based PCs; and you're not all that attracted to what you've seen of the Mac; then get a Windows-based PC. There's more choice, prices are a bit lower, and you'll get the help you need from your friends and family.

If, on the other hand, several of the people around you use a Mac, and you like the style and look of them you see, then get a Mac yourself. You pay a bit more up front, but the machines are exceptionally reliable and better-supported than most Windows-based PCs.

Apple's laptops tend to be attractive, thin and light, and solidly backed by a one-year warranty and support. They connect very well to an Apple iPod or iPhone, if you have one. And you can even get free, in-person, first-level support at an Apple Store.

You'll pay more for an Apple laptop, though, and you're quite likely to be more on your own when it comes to informal support from friends and family. Keep these trade-offs in mind as you make a decision.

Windows 7, the latest version of Windows at the time of writing, has some features that make Windows-based notebooks particularly interesting. These include the ability to run on slightly less hardware, making notebooks more affordable. Windows 7 also has improved power management, so a battery charge may last longer. Windows 7 closes the gap with Mac-based notebooks in these areas.

Windows 7 also has the ability to connect to a built-in GPS device. (GPS stands for Global Positioning System and can tell you where you and your computer are.) For a highly portable computer such as a notebook, knowing where you are could be very cool. It could allow you to find friends, search for a nearby restaurant you'd like and, of course, to get directions to where you're going. The best notebook computers can still give you that 'wow' factor today. They can allow you to have nearly all the power of a larger computer with true portability, allowing you to carry the computer with you throughout the day.

So with all that good news, what could possibly go wrong? The first concern is price. A well-made, full-featured notebook costs from about £400 to £600 (more for a Mac), although prices are gradually decreasing. At the low end, features may not be much more than for a netbook; at the high end, you may be paying more than for a larger laptop for a computer that, while more portable, has fewer features.

Another concern is battery life. Because notebooks are so small and light, you really don't want to compromise the advantages by carrying a power cord and transformer with you. It can be annoying to run out of power when you're having fun, but also can be a pain to have to carry a power cord around with you. The other concern, when choosing a laptop is, ironically, size. The very miniaturisation that makes a notebook easy to carry also makes it somewhat harder to use. It's not as bad as with a netbook, but everything is still compressed – the keyboard and the screen.

Because notebooks are designed to be used on the move, they're typically equipped with a trackpad for moving the cursor around and used without a mouse. (I still recommend one, as it makes moving the cursor around much less fiddly.)

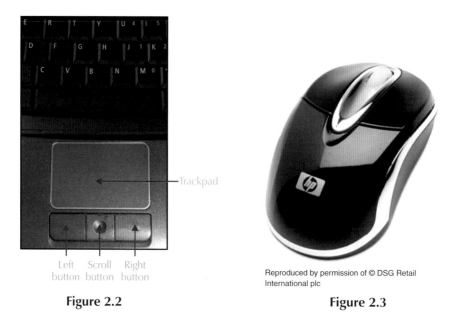

Trackpad

Left   Scroll   Right
button button   button

Figure 2.2

Reproduced by permission of © DSG Retail International plc

Figure 2.3

Notebooks usually have enough storage to store all your software and a fair number of documents, photos, music files and so on. It's all just a bit harder to get at with the screen and keyboard being smaller.

A notebook is still harder to learn on and to use than a larger laptop or a desktop computer. The portability and convenience, though, may make it worthwhile for you.

Using the Vaio as an example

To explore whether a Windows-based notebook computer is right for you, let's take a look at a recent model from Sony's famous Vaio line.

Vaio is an acronym for Video Audio Integrated Operation, and the Vaio line was launched in 1998. The name is meant to suggest multimedia support along with traditional computing. The distinctive Vaio brand marked Sony's re-entry into making computers in the later 1990s.

Reproduced from Sony

Figure 2.4

Let's take a look at a specific model of the Vaio to illuminate what you can expect from a notebook computer. The computer in question is the Sony Vaio VGN-CS215J/W. (Sony and Vaio are well-known names, but the names of specific Vaio models are almost always a confusing mess of letters and numbers.)

Reproduced from Sony

Figure 2.5

The CS215J/W is a slight step up from the lowest-price Vaio sold in shops. It's clean-looking and shiny – much like similar Mac computers.

I'm going to mention some of the detailed specifications here to give you a feel for them. I'll explain them in more detail in the next chapter. However, as with Mac computers, most people who buy a Sony Vaio buy it for its looks and multimedia capabilities rather than on a careful price and feature comparison.

The Vaio has a very nice keyboard and a responsive touch pad. It has 4GB of RAM, which is plenty for any normal daily use, and a 250GB hard drive, which is actually considered a bit on the small size today.

Like most Vaio computers, this one includes multimedia programs for movies, videos and photos. It also includes the add-in programs that go by the name of 'bloatware', trial versions of applications that you have to pay for to use fully. It's left to you to remove them if you care to.

The computer is on the high end of the category in size and weight, with a 14-inch screen and a weight of 5.7 lbs. The screen has a resolution of 1,280 by 800 pixels, which is very common in wide-screen laptops today. Using this resolution on a 14-inch screen means that there's enough space to see everything.

Reproduced from Sony

Figure 2.6

I have a laptop with 1,280 by 800 resolution, and I personally find this resolution frustrating. It's great for wide-screen movies, but I'd prefer to watch those on a television or in a cinema. For looking at Web pages or writing, you can put two windows side by side, which is nice, but each window is a bit short and squat. Try this on the computer you're considering to make the right choice for yourself.

This Vaio is available for about £600 in the shops, a perfectly reasonable price for a nice notebook. With a 14-inch screen and a weight of more than 5 lbs, it's as big as you would want in a computer that you might carry around with you several times a week.

Given that this Vaio is relatively competitive on size, weight and features, how is Sony making any money? The price is a little higher and the hard disk – a crucial component in terms of the price, size and weight of a notebook – is on the small side in terms of capacity. The battery life is also on the low side. Other laptops at a similar price run for longer. Sony also makes about $50 per PC by including bloatware.

If you plan to use your laptop on the move, and feel ready and able to work on a smaller system, you might even consider a 13-inch screen, which might come attached to a computer that weighs 4 to 5 lbs, and would be significantly easier to carry around.

The great thing about notebooks today – any computer with a 14-inch screen or smaller – is that you used to pay a premium for a notebook computer. The Vaio with a 12-inch screen that I had way back when cost about twice what its larger sibling costs today, about £1,500. You were paying extra for miniaturisation. Squeezing a big chipset and big components, such as the hard disk drive, into a small space meant a lot of extra engineering work, as well as some tradeoffs.

One such trade-off was (and still is) heat. Some notebooks from various manufacturers get too hot to sit comfortably in your lap, which is not very good in a computer called a 'laptop'. Another trade-off was features. The graphics in notebook computers were not as good because there was no room for powerful, separate graphics chips. The amount of memory and the hard disk size that could be included were always behind what was available in bigger laptops and desktop machines.

Watch out for cheap notebooks. Read reviews, visit computer shops and ask questions before buying. It's common for notebook PC makers to push systems that seem like a good deal but have one or two flaws, either due to saving money on some component, rushing the engineering work, or both. The Mona Lisa is a beautiful painting, but it wouldn't be quite so beautiful if Leonardo had skimped on paint to save money.

These trade-offs still exist today to some extent. With smaller chipsets, however, and with Windows 7 needing less hardware than Vista did, a fully capable mainstream computer can be squeezed into the form of a notebook without too much strain.

A mainstream notebook computer is almost certainly powerful enough for normal use. Only hard-core computer gamers and people who make long, high-quality movies, burn a lot of DVDs or undertake other demanding tasks are likely to need more than a mainstream notebook computer can offer them.

Make sure the notebook is big enough and well-made enough, with a large enough screen and good enough keyboard that you can actually use it. Then, and only then, see if it's small enough to carry around. Don't choose something that's easy to carry but that you can't do much with when you get there.

It's quite common, among couples, for one partner to drive the buying decision and the other to warm to the computer only later. Make sure the computer you choose can be used by both of you.

Metal or plastic?

There used to be a big difference in look and feel between portable computers made of metal and those made of plastic. The metal ones felt strong and reliable, but were heavy; the plastic ones felt cheap and breakable, but were light.

Now technology has obscured the distinction. Plastics can be made quite stiff, and finishes for plastics can make them seem almost, well, metallic. As a result, plastic has just about taken over the world of laptops. At the same time, metallurgy and machining technology have advanced. The best-made metal laptops are now no heavier than the plastic ones, and still have a feel that plastic can't quite match.

If you particularly need a very strong, yet light laptop, ask about laptops made of metal. (You might not always be able to tell the difference on your own.) Many Windows-based laptops mix metal and plastic parts together, or use metal plates in some areas to stiffen the plastic.

However, don't think a metal or part-metal laptop is automatically tougher in every possible way. To really be tough, a computer needs a special screen. Its internal components need to be shock mounted and the whole thing should be 'ruggedised' against water and fizzy drink spillages and the shock of being dropped or kicked.

The size of a computer screen can make a big difference in how much you enjoy using it. Let's take a look at some numbers to see why this is so.

A screen with a diagonal measurement of 15 inches doesn't sound that much bigger than a screen 13 inches across. In fact, 15 inches is only about 16% more than 13 inches.

But you don't use a computer screen along just one measurement, you use the whole area of it. A 13-inch screen is about 81 square inches in area. A 15-inch screen is about 108 square inches. That's 33%, or one-third, more.

That extra space makes a big difference in how useful a computer is to you, especially if your eyes are no longer as sharp as they used to be. If you suffer any kind of visual impairment, the extra space is vital.

Summary

- Your friends and family are a good source of information and advice.

- The way Windows PCs are made and sold keeps prices low.

- There are many thin, light Windows 7-based laptops to choose from.

- Netbooks, notebooks and full-sized laptops are the main classes of laptop.

- Larger laptops, with 15-inch screens and up, are a good blend of features and transportability.

Brain Training

There may be more than one correct answer to these questions.

1. Who is a good source for advice in choosing a laptop?

a) People your own age

b) People in middle age

c) Young people

d) No one

2. How much does a true netbook weigh?

a) About 1lb, like a hardcover book

b) About 2 lbs

c) About 3 lbs

d) About 5 lbs

3. Which is likely to have the longest battery life?

a) A notebook

b) A mainstream laptop

c) A desktop replacement

d) A netbook

4. Is a laptop more expensive than a desktop?

a) About twice as expensive

b) A little more expensive

c) Prices are the same

d) Laptops are a bit less expensive

5. What is the biggest concern with a laptop vs. a desktop?

a) Cost

b) Losing it

c) Damaging it

d) Having it stolen

Answers

Q1 – a, b and c   **Q2** – b   **Q3** – d   **Q4** – b

Q5 – d

Understanding laptop specifications

3

Equipment needed: access to different laptops to try them out – at a friend's home, in a classroom or at a computer shop.

Skills needed: willingness to press various buttons and flick different switches on, under and behind a computer.

Arguably, the most intimidating aspect of buying a computer these days is not the bill at the end, but the list of specifications for each computer they're considering.

Many years ago, prospective car buyers faced a similar daunting array of components and features when choosing a car: details about the engine, transmission and so on. Gradually, as the focus shifted to things like comfort and fuel consumption, the specifications were taken out of the picture. A similar process is taking place now with computers, but it's just beginning.

Don't worry – you don't need to understand the specifications in any detail, only at a 'big picture' level. To start, keep these three things in mind:

- **Cutting corners**. Many manufacturers will save money by cutting costs on one or two components. You can spot this if you compare specifications between otherwise similar systems.

- **Shock and awe**. Manufacturers will try to dazzle you with one or two specification features beyond the norm, and probably beyond your requirements. Knowing what the specifications mean helps you avoid paying extra for things you don't need.

● **Comfort**. Some of the most important details relating to a laptop's comfort are given as specifications, such as weight. It's nice to know how easy it might be to carry a given laptop with you in your bag for a whole day.

In this chapter I divide specifications up into three groups: first, the parts you can see, which relate mainly to comfort. Next, the parts you can't see, which determine how fast and capable your computer system is. Finally, there's the printer, the most important external device you attach to your computer system.

With this information to hand, you'll be ready to go shopping and make a well-informed purchase.

The parts you can see and feel

Whether we realise this or not, we all make an initial and usually fairly instant judgment of a laptop based on one simple factor: do we like the look? Naturally, for some you will, others you won't, and for reasons that may be hard to understand logically.

Is the appearance very important? Actually, it is. Remember, the goal is to make a purchase you're ultimately happy with. Liking the look of the laptop is certainly an important part of that. It may also indicate the overall care with which the computer has been put together.

When you go shopping for a laptop, the aesthetics of some laptops will grab you more than others. That's a good first step towards being happy with your purchase, but do take the time to look beyond just the appearance.

Here I'll describe the parts of the computer you can see, which should help you understand some of the 'wow factor': the features which help us decide whether we like or dislike a computer on first impression.

When you go into a computer shop, or are looking at a friend's or family member's computer, inspect all of the following:

● The size of the screen.

● The size, thickness, and weight of the computer.

- The materials and finish of the case, both the top and the base.

- The material and finish of the screen.

- The feel and comfort of the keyboard and track pad.

- Whether the computer has a removable battery.

Laptop size and weight

You want a brilliant screen and a comfortable-to-use keyboard and trackpad, and as little additional size and weight as possible.

How much space will a computer take up on your desk (or lap) and in your bag? That's determined by its screen size, the overall size of the laptop when opened up, and its thickness.

Your choice of screen size

There are three major types of laptops:

- **Netbooks**: True netbooks are under 10 inches in screen size and around 2 lbs in weight. A good additional device, but not recommended as a starter system or as a main computer.

- **Notebooks** (some of these are called 'netbooks' as well): 12 to 14 inches in screen size and 3 to 5 lbs in weight. This is often a good choice that combines portability with performance.

- **Full-sized laptops and desktop replacements**: 15 to 17 inches in screen size, or even larger, and 6 lbs or more in weight. Good transportable computers for use mainly in the home, but not as easy to carry around with you a lot.

Types of laptops are largely defined by screen size.

Screen size and desktop space requirements

The amount of space a laptop takes up is almost completely determined by the screen size. The size of the laptop's top is determined by the screen, plus a bit of space around the edges for the plastic that holds the screen in place. (The extra space shouldn't be more than two or three centimetres.) The size of the computer's base, the part that actually sits on the desk, is the same as the laptop's top.

Figure 3.1

If a laptop has a lot of extra plastic around the screen, you may not be getting the full screen size and you may also have to deal with the extra size and weight this creates. Try to avoid laptops with several centimetres of extra plastic all around the screen.

The gold standard for fitting the computer around the screen is the MacBook Pro line, which carries the edge of the screen right up to the edge of the casing itself. The closer a laptop gets to this standard, the better.

Thickness and weight

Once the desktop 'footprint' of your laptop is determined, the only other variable to determine the overall size is its thickness.

Laptops have recently experienced a transition. It used to be that a typical thin laptop was 3-4cm thick at its thickest point, usually near the hinge between the top and the base. But today, laptops are increasingly thin. Apple's MacBook Air, for example, is only three-fourths of an inch (1.9cm) thick at its thickest point, the hinge, tapering to less than a quarter of an inch (4mm) at the front edge. By comparison, many newer PC laptops are 1 inch thick (2.5cm) or less.

This new thinness leads to a reduction in weight as well. The MacBook Air is just 3 lbs (1.36kg), 2 lbs less than a 13-inch MacBook, which weighs 5 lbs (2.26kg). Newer laptops are down from the 5 to 6 lb range to on average 3 to 4 lb, which is an important reduction.

I love the new very thin, light laptops. They slip into a carrying bag very easily and are easy to carry.

Keyboard and trackpad

A trackpad isn't where pole vaulters and hurdlers hang out between meets. It's a rectangle on your laptop's keyboard that you're meant to use to control the cursor, the little arrow that you move around on the screen of your laptop. It is, in effect, the laptop equivalent of the mouse.

Trackpad

Left button Scroll button Right button

Figure 3.2

Not everyone finds it easy to adapt to a trackpad. You can disable your trackpad and buy a mouse to plug into your laptop if you find this easier to use.

The keyboard is the unsung hero of laptops. A good one can make using the computer much easier; a poor one can make it much harder.

There are two main factors regarding keyboards that seem to make the most difference. The first is the overall comfort of typing. For typing to be comfortable, the keys need to be just the right distance apart and yield to a firm press that is neither too hard nor too soft.

Figure 3.3

The size of your hands, the length and strength of your fingers and past experience (or inexperience) with keyboards can all affect what you find comfortable. A keyboard that is great for one person might be unsuitable for someone else.

In addition to overall comfort, the position of a few specific control keys seems to make a big difference to a lot of people. The Shift and Caps Lock keys are especially important, as you use some form of Shift in every sentence, and accidentally TURNING CAPS LOCK ON is one of the most common typing mistakes people make.

If you already use a computer, try comparing your current keyboard to those of the laptops you're considering buying. Your fingers learn the location and spacing of the keys on one computer, so significant differences between one keyboard and another can really slow you down and can be frustrating. Therefore, you may decide to buy a keyboard that's as similar as possible to the one you're used to. Some people even buy successive computers from the same product line to make adapting to such factors easier.

Controls

Your laptop should include easy to find controls for important aspects of the computer. Laptops usually have the following controls, in one form or another:

● **Sound on/off**. There should be a button for quickly turning the sound on and off, because you often want to mute your laptop after previously listening to something. Windows or MacOS will use an icon, usually represented by a small graphical symbol onscreen, to show whether the volume is on or not. However, you may also need an actual physical button, particularly for easy 'off' access.

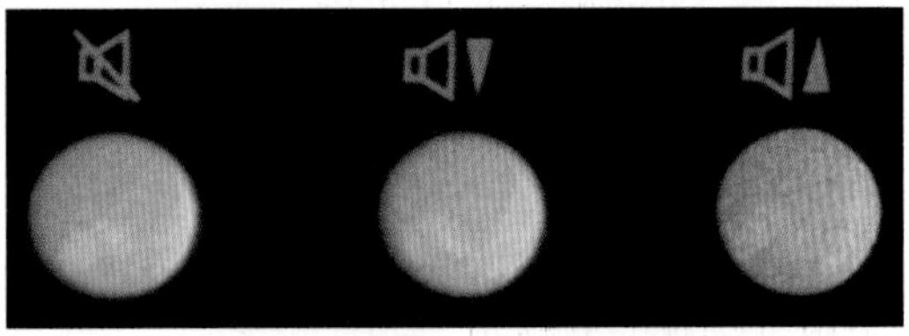

● **Volume control**. There should be easy to find and easy to press buttons for turning the sound down or up. Different programs and websites play sound at completely different

Figure 3.4

volume levels and you need a quick way to turn the sound up or down.

● **Screen brightness**. You need easy to use buttons for making the screen brighter or dimmer. It's often easier on your eyes, and always easier on battery life, to turn the screen brightness down.

● **Page up/Page down and arrow keys**. These keys are a handy alternative to the trackpad or mouse and great for browsing Web pages, for example, as well as long documents.

Figure 3.5

● **Numeric keypad**. If you're used to using number keys on a computer or calculator, you may find you'll really want them on your computer too. Sadly, there usually isn't room on most laptops to accommodate a separate numeric keypad. If this is non-negotiable for you, however, look carefully for a laptop with this feature that still meets your other needs besides.

Figure 3.6

- **Wireless on/off**. I didn't think I needed a wireless network indicator/ control, but my current laptop has one and I love it. I can immediately see if there's a wireless network nearby – if there is, it may well be private and inaccessible to me, but at least I know. And when I'm desperate to save battery power, with the push of a button, I can turn off wireless access and claw back a few crucial minutes of power use. Next time I turn on the computer, I can instantly see that it's turned off and simply click to turn it back on.

What form should these controls take? It is easier to use separate, clearly labelled, dedicated buttons. (In this context, 'Dedicated' means 'only used for one purpose'.) However, sometimes these controls are on the keyboard as shared functions keys. Usually these are numbered F1 to F12, and you might have to press the Function (or Fn) button to use them.

Figure 3.7

When considering a laptop, find the location of these keys and try them.

Figure 3.8

DVD drive

Most laptops today have a DVD drive. You want a DVD drive that can not only play back DVDs, but also write information on them. Since the DVD can hold a lot of information, you can use it to back up data from your computer's hard drive for safekeeping or to send to someone.

At the shop, just ask if the laptop can write DVDs as well as read them. It probably can. You may find a computer that can read or, if you're lucky, even write Blu-Ray disks. Blu-Ray is like DVD, only higher-capacity. This is a nice option to have, but for most of us it's not worth paying extra for.

The location and control of the DVD drive is important. Try inserting and removing a DVD. Make sure the DVD drive is not on the same side or in the way of the power cable or the USB ports.

Most Apple laptops have a DVD drive that is both particularly great and particularly frustrating. It's just a slot in the side of the machine into which you insert the DVD. It pulls the DVD in very smoothly, but there's no way to eject a DVD without using the computer's menus or other commands. If you just want your DVD back without messing with a bunch of onscreen menus or other commands, you might prefer a PC.

Web cam

A web cam is a tiny camera built into your laptop, peeking out along the top edge of the screen. At some point in your experience of using a laptop, you might want to have a live video chat with someone – a friend, a family member, perhaps a grandchild. It's not the same as being there in person, but it definitely beats a phone call. If your computer has a web cam, this will be easy to do. Ask your guardian angel to help you activate the web cam instructions specific to your laptop.

Web cam

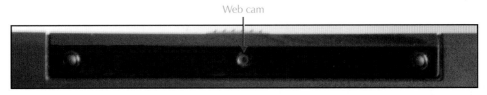

Figure 3.9

Connectors

Those little holes around the edges of a laptop; what are they all for? One is the power connection, and you may also have a connector for an anti-theft device. The rest are connectors or 'ports', for sending and/or receiving information to and from external devices of one kind or another.

Here are the top types of connectors and a few tips on how to use them:

● **USB ports**. The number of USB ports may be the most fought-over feature of laptops today. I have three on my laptop and it's just enough. Most laptops will have 2-4 USB ports, which can be used to connect a variety of hardware including an external mouse, a memory stick or even a printer.

● **Power connector**. The power connector's placement is important as you will want the power cord out of your way. Ideally, the power connector will be at the back edge of the machine or, failing that, at the back edge of one of the sides.

- **Network connector** (also called a 10BaseT connector). This is a connector for a wired network. You rarely need this these days, but it's important to have one nonetheless, just in case.

- **External monitor connection** (also called VGA connector). This allows you to hook up an external monitor to your laptop so you can use it instead of (or as well as) your laptop's built-in screen.

- **Speaker and microphone plugs**. Ideally these should be next to each other on the front of the machine so you can easily plug in a headphones/ microphone combination. Then you can not only listen to music or watch movies in private, but also (using Skype, see Chapter 11), make free phone and even video calls to computer users anywhere in the world, or make cheap international phone calls. Marvellous!

- **Bluetooth interface** (invisible). Bluetooth is a short-range wireless system for enabling devices to talk to each other. On your laptop, you might use Bluetooth to connect wirelessly to a headset, a mobile phone or a printer.

- **Wireless connector** (invisible). The wireless connector is a sort of radio that 'tunes in' to local wireless signals to connect your laptop to the Internet. You might sometimes see this referred to as '802-11g/n' from time to time.

- **Memory card reader**. Cameras, mobile phones, and other consumer electronics devices sold today use memory cards that are quite small and cost tens of pounds each. They are easy to lose, along with your precious contact information or photographs. A memory card reader is probably just useful enough that you should insist on having one on your laptop.

- **Video connectors**. There are different video interfaces, with names that include S-Video, DVI and HDMK, which allow faster connectivity to a movie camera or high-definition television, for instance.

Figure 3.10

These ports are not labelled, and some of them are similarly shaped, making it quite easy to put in the wrong plug into the wrong connector. There's almost never any harm done, though, and eventually you'll figure out what to plug in where.

Removable battery

A small but growing number of laptops have non-removable batteries.

Figure 3.11

Look on the bottom of any computer you're considering and see if the battery is removable. If it is, you'll see a crease between the battery and the rest of the computer and a catch for freeing the battery and removing it. Try it – you won't break anything. (Don't drop the battery, though; they're heavy, about a pound in weight, and can be awkward to handle.)

The parts you can't see

Understanding the guts of a computer, the parts you can't see, is a little harder than the exterior features. Thinking about laptop specifications reminds me of a story about two hikers and a bear. Two hikers reached a stream and took off their shoes and backpacks to rest a bit. Suddenly, downstream a quarter of a mile, they saw a bear. The bear hunkered down on all fours and started running towards them.

One of the hikers reached into his backpack, pulled out a pair of running shoes and started putting them on. The other hiker said, sardonically, 'Even with running shoes, you're not going to outrun a bear.'

The hiker with the running shoes said, 'I don't need to outrun a bear. I just need to outrun you.'

It's the same with computer internals. You just need to know enough to protect your interests better than most people out there. You don't need to know the gory details.

Internal components

Internal components are the 'guts' of the computer. Computer performance used to be largely determined by a few key variables such as microprocessor speed and hard disk size and speed. Today most computers are 'good enough' for most uses, and as such, these details are less important.

Here are the top few of the most important components inside your computer:

Figure 3.12

- **Microprocessor**. This is the brains of a computer. Most microprocessors today can handle all that a mainstream user is likely to throw at them. The two major manufacturers are Intel and AMD. If your laptop has either, you are probably in the clear.

- **RAM (Random Access Memory)**. This is the fast memory that the microprocessor manipulates to make things happen on your computer. Two gigabytes (2GB) of RAM is enough for most routine work. If a laptop has more than 2GB of RAM it's a nice bonus and I always recommend as much RAM as fits the budget.

- **Hard disk drive**. A 250GB hard drive should be enough for most users. However, remember the manufacturer will have used some of the space already with programs they have installed along with the operating system.

Ask how much free space is available on the hard drive when you buy the laptop; you should have at least 100GB available for yourself.

- **Video processor and video memory**. If your laptop plans mostly involve using the Internet, email, and word processing, you can probably live with no separate video processor and shared video memory. Many laptops may have a shared video memory and no separate video processor but you don't necessarily need that.

Wasting time with your laptop

One of my main points in this book is that most mainstream laptops have all the performance that typical users need; yet computer users spend plenty of time waiting for their computers to do things. Wouldn't a high-end computer be faster?

The answer, perhaps surprisingly, is usually no. Windows may not start up noticeably quicker on a faster system. Many of the delays in normal computer startups are caused by the system carrying out myriad checks against virus infections and so on, which don't necessarily run that much faster with faster hardware. Many Web pages won't load any quicker, because it's actually data transmission over the Internet that is slowing things down. Your laptop's speed will have no impact on that.

High-performance computers today are like high-performance cars; they won't get you out of a traffic jam any quicker, and the motorways have speed limits and speed cameras to enforce regulations. In many cases, the extra performance of a computer is more about making the buyer feel good rather than actually getting useful things done noticeably faster.

A high-performance computer might, for example, burn a lot of data to a DVD drive faster, but you're only likely to do this once in a while, and you'll do something else while you wait anyway. What's the difference if the wait is long enough to inspire a tea break anyway?

Nowadays, the only people who routinely push computers to the maximum are those who frequently use the graphics subsystem – primarily graphic designers and hard-core gamers. Most ordinary people watching a video, surfing the Web and so on are, in my opinion, well served by a mainstream system.

'Moore's Law' is perhaps the most famous rule in computing. More of an observation than a law, this is a statement by Gordon Moore, one of the founders of Intel, that the power of computer chips doubles roughly every year and a half. Moore's Law has generally held for several decades and has led to ever more powerful and inexpensive computers.

Included Software

It's hard to prescribe rules on how best to approach included software. It changes from one system to another, and can change over time on any given system. Many systems tout extras like 60 day trial versions of antivirus software.

To be completely honest, you may find that you won't use any pre-added software. More on this in Chapter 6.

Figure 3.13

Before you buy, you need to know that there are three notable exceptions:

1. **Windows 7**. Microsoft follows the practice of selling different versions of Windows 7 for different prices, requiring you to figure out just what you do or don't need. The vast majority of laptops include Windows 7 Home Premium or Home Basic. The more superior the version of Window 7 you can get, the better, but don't pay extra for the upgrade.

2. **Microsoft Office**. There are just too many files out there that work with these programs, and too many people using them, to consider going without. If it's included in a system for free, that's a nice plus.

3. **MacOS and included software**. Macs come with low-end versions of programs somewhat like those in Office, plus multimedia software that is actually usable by mere mortals. Windows PCs have more basic multimedia software for free as well.

Otherwise, included software is largely to be avoided as opposed to sought after. Try to get a laptop with as little as possible.

Figure 3.14

Printer specifications

There's only one other piece of hardware that you really should buy along with your laptop, if you don't already have it, and that's a printer.

There are plenty of inexpensive inkjet printers for around £50 or even less that will do the job for you. They print several pages a minute in black and white or colour. The quality of printers and the cost of ink varies significantly, though, so check reviews carefully before buying.

Inexpensive inkjet printers will do a so-so job of printing photographs. You may want a photo-capable printer, with special paper and special ink. Producing your own photos can be a lot of fun, but it's expensive, both to buy the printer and to buy paper and supplies. It can be cheaper, though less convenient and fun, to have your local photo processing shop print photos for you.

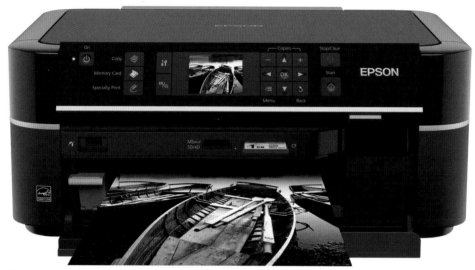

Reproduced by permission of Epson

Figure 3.15

I suggest you just get the best inexpensive inkjet printer you can afford and bring it home with you the day you buy the laptop. If, at a later stage, you want something with more capacity or with photo capability, buy it as an add-on, and use the inexpensive inkjet for simple jobs or for travelling with your computer.

Summary

- The screen size is the key factor that determines a laptop's size and weight.

- Laptop cases are mostly plastic, some having metal mixed in; a few are all-metal.

- The feel and arrangement of the keyboard are critical to your happiness with a laptop.

- USB ports are the most useful connectors for your computer.

- Important internal components include the microprocessor, the amount of RAM and the hard disk drive size (perhaps 150 to 500GB).

- An inexpensive ink-jet printer is great for starting out with your laptop.

Brain Training

There may be more than one correct answer to these questions.

1. What mostly determines a laptop's overall size?

a) The screen size

b) The brand name

c) The microprocessor type

d) The hard disk size

2. How much should you know about specifications?

a) Nothing

b) Enough to make sure you're getting a good deal

c) Enough to make sure a laptop will be right for you

d) More than anyone else around you

3. What's the least number of USB ports to look for in a laptop?

a) One

b) Two

c) Three

d) Four

4. Which can be somewhat of a waste of money in a laptop?

a) Speaker and microphone in/out connectors

b) A built-in Web cam

c) A DVD drive

d) None

5. How much RAM do you need in a mainstream laptop?

a) 1GB

b) 2GB

c) 3GB

d) 4GB

Answers

Q1 – a   **Q2** – b and c   **Q3** – c   **Q4** – d

Q5 – b

Buying your laptop

Equipment needed: Cash, or a debit or credit card. Optional: if buying online, computer and Internet access.

Skills needed: The ability to keep a cool head and a firm grip on your wallet when you start to get a bit excited about possibly buying the latest and greatest, if that's not what you need.

Actually buying your laptop is an exciting experience. You want to get the best laptop for you, with the fewest potential problems, and the best possible support if glitches occur.

This chapter follows a 'ready, set, go' approach to the process. First, you prepare for the process by setting your budget, including the purchase price and any monthly bills that go with it. You also learn about the different advantages of shopping online for a laptop versus finding one in the shops.

I then take you through the actual purchase process, showing you how to avoid expensive last minute add-ons and overpriced financing offers while protecting your purchase.

Broadband options is a key ingredient for a successful laptop experience. If you already have broadband, or you get mobile broadband as part of your PC purchase, you may not have to concern yourself with it further. The options are discussed in Chapter 5, but keep broadband in mind as you go through this chapter.

The prices and specifics given in this chapter will no doubt shift over time, and the details will be different if you're reading this outside the UK as well. My hope is that by getting right down to the detail level as things stand at the time of writing, I can arm you to make a good purchase that you'll be happy about for a long time to come.

Setting your budget

Before you begin the computer-buying process, I suggest that you set a budget for your purchase. The best way to do this is by a combination of what you can afford and what you should expect to get for your money. Don't buy more than you can afford, and don't spend more than you need to, even if you have the money.

At the time of writing, laptops can range from £350 for an entry level Windows PC, to around £1300 for a top of the line MacBook. Of course there are many, many more options at various price points in between, all based on those specifications we discussed in Chapter 3.

There are a few other costs to keep in mind when thinking about your budget. You will very likely want to surf the Internet with your new laptop. You may get a broadband offer as part of your laptop purchase, but if not, you should expect to spend around £10 per month.

Depending on the software that comes with your new laptop, you may want to consider adding these essential items. Antivirus programs are a must for Windows PCs, and you can pick up a commercial subscription for about £50 per year. There are also several good free antivirus options such as Avira and AVG which can be downloaded from the Internet at no charge.

Most of us will end up using some sort of word processing or spreadsheet program along the way. Microsoft Office is the standard for both Windows PCs and Macs and can be picked up for as little as £70. The completely free Open Office (**www.openoffice.org**) is compatible with Microsoft Office and is a good choice as well, but it doesn't do quite as much.

Reproduced by permission of © 2009 AVG Technologies, formerly Grisoft

Figure 4.1

And finally, if you plan to use your home broadband Internet connection without the bother of wires (and that is one reason why you wanted a laptop in the first place, isn't it?) you will need to purchase a wireless router. Depending on your broadband provider, this magical little device may be included in your subscription. If not, a typical wireless router costs about £40.

So set your budget with all this in mind. The first place where you can easily save money is the cost of the laptop itself. The other way you can save money is by being disciplined and not buying extras that may tempt you. For example, a new laptop bag is nice, but you may already have a bag that will work perfectly well for carrying your new computer.

Reproduced by permission of © DSG Retail International plc

Figure 4.2

You may want to consider buying your laptop in a bundle with mobile broadband. You can do this either in a PC shop, as described later in this chapter, or by looking for the mobile broadband service first, as described in Chapter 5.

Shopping online for a laptop

There are many online sites through which you can buy a computer, many of them offering various choices along the way. The benefit of buying online is the convenience of not having to go to the high street shops to make your purchase. Sometimes laptops purchased online cost a bit less as well, but shipping charges may quickly do away with the savings.

Online shopping has its disadvantages as well. For example, when you shop online, the only indication of a laptop's fit and finish is the photo provided by the website. Similarly, you do not have the opportunity to touch the keyboard, see the display quality, or try the trackpad. And of course a salesperson is usually not available to assist with an online purchase.

Look out for shipping charges when ordering online. Sometimes charges can be very high.

You will need to decide for yourself if purchasing online is right for you. At the very least, window shopping online may help you to narrow your choices before you visit a high street shop – or vice versa. I often use a shop's website to browse the models before I visit.

Typically, stores and their online sites offer a variety of options from the top manufacturers. Others may offer lesser known brands or even specialty brands for very specific uses. If this is your first purchase, may I suggest you first consider a brand you may have heard of before such as HP, Dell, or IBM. In addition, I recommend you begin your search with some of the larger online sellers such as:

- PC World (**www.pcworld.co.uk**)

- Dixons (**www.dixons.co.uk**)

- Amazon (**www.amazon.co.uk**)

You also have the option of using online sites to customise a laptop completely to your liking. The best example of this is Dell's website **www.dell.co.uk**. Buying a laptop from this site is more akin to building a custom laptop for yourself. You start with a base model, and add or remove features until you have the laptop exactly as you like it.

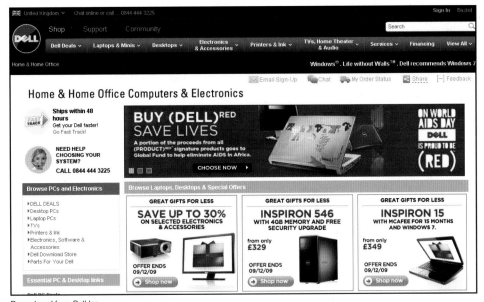

Reproduced from Dell Inc.

Figure 4.3

Of course this has the benefit of allowing you to purchase exactly what you want – either with or without all the extra features. The downside is that it is a bit more complicated than buying 'off the shelf' and you need to deal with those pesky specifications we discussed in Chapter 3 at a slightly greater level of detail.

When buying a laptop online, or any kind of screen or monitor, you can't evaluate the quality of the screen display. Look up some reviews of the model you're considering to check for any possible comments specifically about screen quality before making your purchase.

What about a Mac?

You can shop online for a Mac just as you can for a Windows PC. The online Apple store offers you fewer choices than the Dell site.

If you want a Mac, don't be afraid to buy it online if you have an Apple store nearby; you can get first-line support at the Apple store no matter where you buy. If, however, your only Apple outlet is a local Apple dealer, you may want to buy your Mac there rather than online, as they are likely to provide support if you buy from them.

Finding a laptop in the shops

Over the years, I have accumulated quite a bit of knowledge and perspective on laptops. I've had a laptop of one sort or another for the past 20 years now. I have even worked for both Apple and Microsoft. Still, with all that experience, I'd generally rather buy a laptop in a shop than online. You just don't get the hands-on 'feel' for such a complex purchase with an online site, even if you know laptops well.

Shopping in a computer store means you have a place to take the computer to when there are problems and real people you can speak to about it. Many issues are handled quickly and efficiently, especially if any problems arise shortly after purchase.

PC manufacturers constantly change model designations to make it hard to compare in-store and online offers and to find reviews on the model you might actually want to buy. Be persistent in researching not only name brands, but also specific, well-known models for which you can find reviews and price comparisons, online or in print.

Look and feel

Begin your shopping experience by examining the look and feel of various machines. The keyboard is a great starting point. Memorise a sample sentence or two to type. ('The quick brown fox jumped over the lazy red dogs' has every letter in the alphabet in it.) Which keyboard is comfortable for you? What's the smallest keyboard, and therefore the smallest machine you feel comfortable with?

Don't be afraid to ask for a chair and somewhere to sit while you try typing, the way you'll be using the laptop in real life. Computer shops are set up for only a brief look at a machine, but you need a real feel for it, which only comes with slightly longer exposure.

If you have smaller hands, you might be able to make good use of the small keyboards that come with screens with 13-inch systems. However, you may prefer a larger keyboard such as those which come with a 15-inch screen. You may find you want the extra function keys, a separate numeric keypad and so on, that are found only on laptops with a 17-inch screen or a desktop system.

Next, check out the screen. One common use of a laptop is to look up something on the Web while writing a document, such as an email or letter, alongside it. As an experiment, try having a word processing document and a Web page, such as a news website, open next to each other. Type a few words from the website into the document, and then navigate to a different Web page. Type a bit more. Is the screen large and bright enough to support you in this kind of simulated work?

 While trying out the laptops in-store, don't sign into any sites that display personal information in public, such as your bank account or medical details. People are all too ready to look over your shoulder and see what you're doing.

See if you're able to move the cursor around the screen easily, whether with the trackpad or a mouse. If you watch people use the trackpad, you'll see most of them stop typing for a brief period while they move the cursor around. With a mouse, moving the cursor is faster and requires less concentration.

Now compare screens. Pull up the same website on two screens and read from both. One screen may be brighter than the other, which is a good thing only if the text displayed onscreen is still sharp and clear.

Having assessed the laptop from the 'inside out', i.e. from a user's perspective, now check it out from the 'outside in' that is, by carrying it around. Fold the screen closed and pick up the machine. Does it feel light enough to carry comfortably, or is it a bit heavy for you? Is another machine nearby more comfortable?

Unless you're certain that you need a Windows PC, try the same exercises on a Mac. Do you like the look and feel of the Mac more or less?

Specifications

You need to look at the specifications for a computer to make sure you're getting a good deal. Also, once you have specifications for the computer you're considering in the shops, you can compare a Mac vs. a Windows PC, or an in-store Windows PC to one you can purchase on a website, to make sure you're getting everything you need and that you're getting a good deal.

If you are buying your laptop online, you can often find product specifications beside the product. They may look similar to figure 4.4.

This gives you all the key details about your potential laptop.

Unlike the customised systems you might purchase from websites like Dell, those available in retail outlets are already configured. You have to buy what's on offer; if the system you like comes with a 250GB hard drive, and you'd be just as happy with 160GB, there's no way to downgrade and recoup any savings. You have to settle for a system close to your ideal specifications and price.

Use a checklist like the one shown later in this chapter to compare systems. The checklist is partially filled in with specifications for a system that I would suggest to most users interested in typical home computing.

Details | Reviews

- Intel Atom N270 processor.
- 1.60GHz processor speed.
- 1GB DDR2 RAM.

- 10.1in screen size.
- Resolution 1024 x 600 pixels.
- 160GB hard drive.

- Intel GMA 950 shared graphics.
- Multi card reader.

- 3 x USB ports.
- LAN 10/100/ fast Ethernet.
- Built-in digital microphone.
- Built-in speakers.

- 0.3MP webcam.
- Wireless LAN 802.11b/g.

- Microsoft Windows XP Home edition.

- Software included:
- Microsoft Works Office Home and Student 2007 (trial version), McAfee internet security suite (60 day trial version), Adobe Reader, Adobe Flash Player, eSobi, Carbonite online backup, Windows Live Essentials Wave 3, Video Conference Manager 4.0.

- 3 hours battery life.
- Size (H)2.54 (W)25.85, (D)18.4cm.
- Weight 1.2kg.

Reproduced from Argos limited 2009 ©

Figure 4.4

It's fine to vary from these recommendations, but make sure you know why you're doing it. For instance, if you get a small-screen system instead of the recommended 15 inch size, make sure you are able to get the most out of the smaller keyboard and can easily see what's happening on a smaller screen. If you get extra RAM or a bigger hard disk, know how you're going to benefit from the extra cost involved.

	Recommended Windows PC	System 1	System 2
Screen size	15 inch widescreen		
Resolution	1280 × 800		
CPU	2 GHz dual-core, power saving		
RAM	2GB		
Hard drive	160GB		
Graphics	Integrated		
Battery	6-cell		
DVD drive	DVD read/write		
Wireless Internet	Included		
Bluetooth support	Included		
WebCam	Integrated, no additional charge		
OS	Windows 7 Home Premium/ current MacOS version		
Virus protection	£40-£50 for at least one year (Windows only)		

The deal

Use the specifications comparison chart to see what kind of a deal you're getting.

The competition between laptops and desktop computers is intense. As a result, some salespeople might want to rush you through the laptop purchase, only to switch their focus to selling you various add-ons. If you encounter this, no matter where you're buying or however persuasive the sales talk may sound, resist it. Your core purchase is the actual laptop, and I suggest you concentrate on that bit first.

Shops also tend to want to sell bundles and combinations of products. If you really need the other products, this can be worthwhile. For instance, mobile broadband and laptop bundles can be a good deal, as discussed below. However, adding on products that are only marginally connected, such as a television or even a digital camera, is rarely a good idea in my opinion.

So keep steering the salesperson back to the laptop, perhaps a printer if you need one, and a few pieces of software that you really need on Day 1. By this time they are likely to want to close the sale and may offer you a good deal.

Also use consumer advice websites such as **www.which.co.uk**. This website gives unbiased advice on a range of products. Just enter 'laptop reviews' in the search box and it will display a range of reviews which might be a useful tool. (To access full reviews, you need to subscribe.) Or, if you want to, look up a specific brand name and find a review. It might provide you with more insight into your chosen laptop, helping you make an informed decision.

Service and support options

A shop or online site may try to sell you all manner of service and support options, above and beyond the few months of phone support and one-year limited warranty on the computer itself that most of them offer.

Buyers may be nervous about their purchase and find these options very attractive. While there's a variety of problems you might come across with a laptop, it will rarely be exactly the problem covered by whatever service and support option you paid for.

I suggest you avoid these service and support add-ons and instead do two things:

● In the first few weeks of ownership, make sure your laptop does everything it's supposed to do. If there are any problems, don't delay; get in touch with the vendor and get the problem fixed.

● Once you get beyond the initial free service and support period and your warranty, pay for service and support when you need it. Over time, it's usually cheaper to pay only for what you need rather than to pre-pay against problems that may never happen.

Laptop and mobile broadband offers

Bundles including a laptop and mobile broadband are popular these days. They are a good option for you to consider if:

- You don't have home broadband yet, and . . .

- You don't need home broadband to share with additional computers at your home, and . . .

- You get a strong mobile broadband signal at home so mobile broadband meets all your broadband needs, and . . .

- You plan to use your laptop on the go often enough that the convenience of mobile broadband is valuable to you.

If all these considerations apply to you, consider bundling the laptop you choose with mobile broadband. The next chapter describes what to look for.

 Users who already have home broadband may find mobile broadband quite costly compared to how often you actually use it.

Paying up

Many stores and online sites offer easy credit terms, and you may want to consider paying with a credit card. You can ask in store for payment options or this information can be found on websites under 'payment methods', or a similar title. This might make sense for you as there are large up-front costs, especially for a first computer purchase. However, a typical laptop only lasts a few years, and there are ongoing costs such as broadband service and virus protection. So be sure that you can pay off the overall purchase comfortably, well within the laptop's anticipated useful life.

There's one final thing to consider if you don't have broadband yet. It can take some time between placing a broadband order and actually having it available. You do want to have your laptop home and ready to use when broadband is activated so you can immediately test it and get it working on your new laptop.

Figure 4.5

Be sure to keep the original purchase receipt for your computer in a safe place. You'll need it to prove the warranty start date if you have problems later. You may also need it for insurance purposes, if the laptop is stolen or damaged; and for tax purposes, if you use the laptop for work and can claim part or all of the expense on your tax return.

Comparing to a Mac

We can use the checklist to compare the price of a Windows laptop to a Mac laptop. The comparison is a bit unfair, as Apple doesn't really 'do' lower-end systems we're using as a price comparison; Apple is more competitive in the mid-range and high end. (Sony and some other vendors are the same, and most vendors, including Apple and Dell, offer business-oriented laptops that cost hundreds of pounds more.) However, it's illuminating to do the comparison, whilst recognising that it's a bit unfair.

We can't exactly compare 'Apples to apples', as Apple doesn't offer a consumer MacBook with a 15-inch screen. Instead, we have to compare the regular MacBook, which has a 13-inch screen – too small for many of us. However, if you were to consider a 13-inch screen laptop, the MacBook has about as large a keyboard and as readable a screen as you might hope for, and it has the lower weight and easy portability you would expect in a smaller laptop.

Otherwise, the specifications for the MacBook meet or exceed the recommendations from the checklist. It has 1280 × 800 screen resolution, a 2GHz Intel dual-core power-saving processor, 2GB of RAM, a separate graphics processor and video RAM (above the recommendations), a 160GB hard disk, a DVD read/write drive, a 6-cell battery with Apple's excellent power management technology, wireless support, Bluetooth support and an integrated web cam.

Reproduced by permission of © DSG Retail International plc

Figure 4.6

The price of a MacBook with these specifications is around £830 at the time of writing. The Apple system also includes multimedia software, so if that is important to you, you won't need to purchase anything additional. However, if you buy Microsoft Office Home and Student for the Mac, you're looking at £110 rather than £70 for the Windows version.

You can use many of the same printers and hardware add-ons for the Mac as for Windows PCs, so prices for add-ons are the same. However, if you shop in the Apple Store, the shelves are largely stocked with premium products that come at a premium price; to save money, get your add-ons at a computer shop that sells both Windows PCs and Macs. Make sure the add-ons you buy have the needed software, called 'drivers', for the Mac; many do, but some don't. Ask the salesperson for assistance.

The total price of the smaller Mac, with slightly better specifications, is higher than the PC laptop. Many people consider this worthwhile. The market share of the Mac has been growing, and Apple does many things right. However, most people buy what the people around them have, which is more likely to be a PC. If you have a guardian angel who is willing to help, consider buying the same kind of system they have.

Summary

- Buying your laptop is an exciting experience, but it can be a little daunting too.

- Arm yourself with information by going through the buying process on a highly ranked online vendor such as Dell and by visiting shops and asking questions.

- Compare the laptops you like by their 'look and feel' as well as screen size, RAM, hard disk size and so on.

- Resist most of the extras that are offered to you and make a purchase you can live with: a quality laptop, the add-ons and software you need to make use of it, all at a reasonable price.

Brain Training

There may be more than one correct answer to these questions.

1. What extra warranties and guarantees should you buy?

a) Accident insurance for the first year

b) A second year's extension to the warranty

c) None

d) Insurance for my mouse and for my cat as well

2. What are total first year costs for a new laptop?

a) Close to £500

b) Close to £1000

c) Close to £1500

d) No cost with broadband wireless access

3. What should you buy with your laptop?

a) An iPod

b) A printer

c) A digital video camera

d) A mouse

4. What are important things to keep?

a) The laptop's documentation

b) CD-ROMs or DVDs that come with the laptop

c) The receipt

d) The original packaging

Answers

Q1 – c   **Q2** – b   **Q3** – b and d

Q4 – a, b, c and d

PART II
Setup

Isn't that _exquisite_, darling...

©2009 Stephen Long

Buying broadband

5

Equipment needed: If possible, computer and Web access for researching broadband suppliers online.

Skills needed: Good judgement to avoid overbuying; perhaps ask family and friends for advice on what they use – they can be a great resource.

Broadband Internet access is considered a national resource in most countries today, just like the electrical grid or the roads network. You should have broadband access in your area already; if not, it's probably on schedule to be provided soon. Check with friends or local government if you don't know the state of broadband access in your area.

Some people still use dial-up access, which is generally much slower, so it can sometimes not be the most viable option. It's like trying to handle a family's daily road transport needs using a scooter: a few people can do it, but most opt for a car. Broadband can make using the Web much easier and allows time- and money-saving options such as making phone calls over the Internet at very low rates, especially for international calls, as described in Chapter 7.

An alternative that business users have had for years, that's finally becoming affordable for consumers – if only barely – is mobile broadband. This kind of Internet access uses the same technology as mobile phones to provide you Internet access. It tends to work well where mobile phones do – that is, out and about in many places – and poorly where mobile phones work poorly, such as in many homes.

You can use mobile phones from various providers as a kind of digital dowsing rod to see whether you 'have signal' for mobile phones and mobile broadband in your house. If you do, mobile access may be the only Internet access you need; if not, you'll need traditional broadband for your home, and perhaps mobile access if you also want wireless access on the move.

Most people, though, will still opt for home broadband as their basic broadband package. It serves the needs of several computers in a home and is relatively inexpensive and fast. You can get home broadband for about £10 a month, or in a package deal with phone and possibly TV service that brings the price down even more.

Focus on getting a good broadband deal, though. Only consider package deals if they include things you really need, at a lower price than you could get otherwise. Don't be afraid to shop around for the right deal before deciding. Prices are competitive and it's all about getting the right deal that will meet your requirements.

The timing on buying broadband service can be confusing. There's usually a wait of a week or two between ordering your broadband service and getting it installed. If you're certain you're going to get a laptop, it's good to get a head start by ordering your home broadband service first, then timing the laptop buy for just after the home broadband service is installed.

If you buy mobile broadband service, though, you either get that in a package with your laptop, as I'll describe below, or immediately after you get your laptop.

 If you want both home broadband and mobile broadband you may be able to get a combination deal for a lower price.

Choosing a broadband provider

The availability of home broadband service from various providers can be found, along with offers from each, using one of several popular web sites. These sites, and the availability of other online information for making your broadband choice, are so useful that I suggest you go online to research this even if you don't yet have a computer or experience in using a computer.

Get a friend, family member, or your guardian angel to help if at all possible. Use your contact's computer, an Internet café or a system at your local library.

There are several widely used 'broadband finders' in the UK; if you live in a different country, use an online search engine such as Google to find one for your country. Here are a few top sites for the UK:

● **Confused.com**, a popular price comparison website, at **www.confused.com**

● Broadband Finder at **www.broadband-finder.co.uk**

● UK Broadband Finder at **www.ukbroadbandfinder.com**

When buying home broadband or mobile broadband online, you don't have to answer all the questions and complete your purchase on the website if you don't want to. On most websites you might use to buy broadband, you can do it by phone or by live online chat as well.

What do the terms mean?

There are several important terms you need to understand before choosing a broadband package:

● **Light, medium and heavy users**. You can surf the Web and send email nearly every waking hour and still be a light user. Medium and heavy users send and receive email with a lot of large files as attachments, play online computer games and/or share music or video files online, even though this last is not always legal.

● **Speed**. The maximum speed of your connection is given in megabits per second (Mbps). The actual speed you achieve may vary, but almost all providers are fast enough to support email, Web surfing and even online phone calls.

- **Download limit**. This can be a limitation for heavier users, who may find they go over their download limit and suddenly unable to download anything more. Your provider will usually alert you if you are exceeding their limitations. However, light users will rarely find themselves going over even a seemingly low limit such as 3GB per month.

- **Setup cost**. This is an initial fee at sign-on.

- **Contract period**. This is how long you're obligated to pay. As with mobile phones, you have to pay through your entire contract period no matter what happens to you and no matter how your needs or the market change.

- **Monthly cost**. The monthly charge you owe throughout the contract period. Watch out for initially discounted 'teaser' rates that obscure the real cost.

You should know what the key terms mean before you buy anything, but if you are just going to use the Web and email and make some online phone calls, you probably don't have to worry much about most of the limitations of a broadband package. Just concentrate on the lowest average cost per month during the contract.

Like mobile phone providers, broadband providers make a lot of their money from people who don't shop around for a new, better deal as soon as their contract ends. Always set up reminders of when your contract ends so you can look for a better deal.

Choosing home broadband

Rather than getting both, you may be able to choose between home broadband and mobile broadband as your only broadband access (and only broadband cost). Here are the tradeoffs:

- **Home broadband**. Home broadband is necessary if you have a desktop computer or plan to get one, or if mobile phone signal strength is weak in your home. It's also desirable if you'll have visitors who have laptops and don't have mobile broadband for them. (Most people today don't.) Home broadband offers unlimited data transfers, or nearly unlimited, so even several users should have plenty of capacity in your home at no extra charge.

- **Mobile broadband**. Mobile broadband as your only broadband access is an option if you don't have, or plan to get, a desktop system, and if you have good mobile phone signal strength in your home. Mobile broadband is often bundled with a laptop in attractive deals, though this may come with tight limits on data transfer per month. Even if you need home broadband, you may still want to get mobile broadband as well for use on the go, or to get a laptop package, though paying for both types of broadband at once is expensive.

Home broadband offers can be confusing. Many of them include low initial 'teaser' monthly payment rates, then a higher rate later.

In the example below, I've used Confused.com because it seems to have the right kind of flexibility for use here and because it displays teaser rates clearly. Feel free to use any broadband package comparison site that seems to meet your needs for researching your options.

Follow these steps to find home broadband access in your area:

1. Open a Web browser.

2. Go to Confused.com at **www.confused.com**.

3. Under Utilities, choose Broadband.

   The Compare Broadband page will appear.

4. Enter your postcode and choose whether you want to look at all packages, bundles or broadband only. Click Search.

   For this example, I've chosen broadband only. After you click Search, a range of options will appear. The choices are sorted by annual cost.

5. To change the sort order, use the dropdown tab, as shown in the figure, to choose the field you want to sort by.

   The choices will reorder by the field you've chosen.

6. Click on a link under the column headed Package details to get details on the package.

   A window will pop up with details of the package.

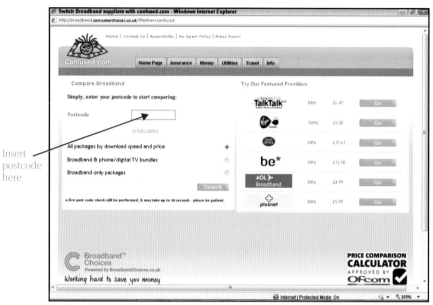

Insert
postcode
here

Reproduced by permission of Confused.com. All rights reserved

Figure 5.1

Sort search results here

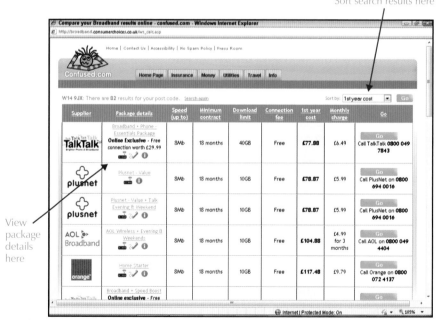

View
package
details
here

Reproduced by permission of Confused.com. All rights reserved

Figure 5.2

I think there can be value in going with a provider you or your friends or family have heard of before, as such a provider may be more likely to be around for the long term. Plusnet is a low-priced provider that comes with the reassurance that it's owned by BT, so you might consider Plusnet alongside the 'big names' that you know and trust like BT itself, Tiscali or Virgin.

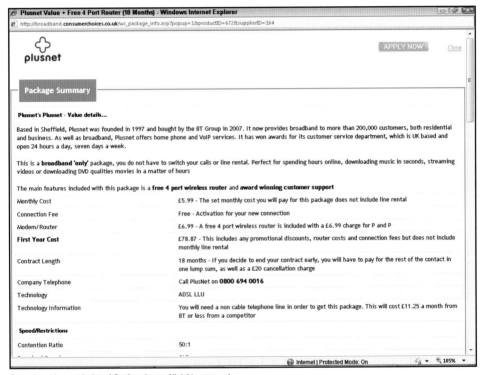

Reproduced by permission of Confused.com. All rights reserved

Figure 5.3

7. Print the details of the package you want, or write them down.

    You'll want these details for later reference and any further comparisons you decide to do.

8. If you want to proceed to order, click the Apply Now button.

I recommend that you give yourself a 'cooling off' period before making a decision. Also, you should consider mobile broadband providers before making a decision. Once you do make a decision, click the Apply Now button; you'll be redirected to the provider's website.

Before ordering, compare the option you've chosen to available offers from your home phone provider (usually BT, in the UK), mobile phone provider (if any) and cable or satellite TV provider (if any). Also consider using the bundles comparison tool, named TV, Broadband & Phone Bundles, on the home page of the Confused.com website.

Choosing a mobile broadband provider

You may want mobile broadband as your only broadband connection or as an 'on the go' service in addition to home broadband (more on this in Chapter 9). To use mobile broadband as your only connection, make sure it works in your home. You can do an initial test using a mobile phone supported by the service provider you're considering.

Top speeds and download limits tend to be lower for mobile broadband deals than for home broadband, but this is unlikely to affect you if you are a light user.

Whether it's your only broadband connection or in addition to home broadband service, you'll want to evaluate any mobile broadband service carefully. Unfortunately, the Confused.com site does not include mobile broadband deals at the time of writing this book. For our example of shopping for a mobile broadband offering, we'll use Broadband Finder.

Follow these steps to find mobile broadband offerings using Broadband Finder:

1. Open a Web browser.

2. Go to Broadband Finder at **www.broadband-finder.co.uk**.

3. Look for the Mobile Broadband area (not the Compare Broadband area, that's for home broadband) and click the Compare button.

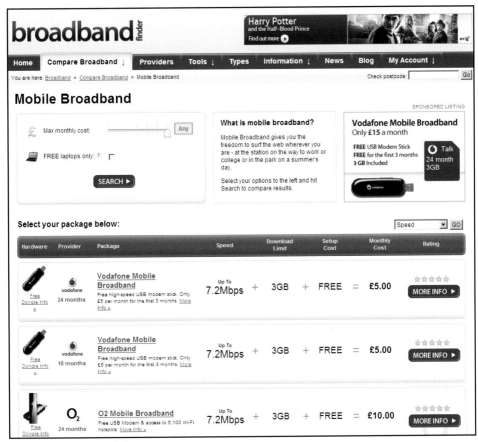

Reproduced from Broadband Finder

Figure 5.4

The Mobile Broadband page will appear.

4. To change the sort order, use the dropdown tab to choose the field you want to sort by. Then click the Go button to re-sort the options.

The choices will reorder by the field you've chosen.

5. Click on a More Info link under the column headed Rating to get details on the package.

A window will pop up with details of the package.

Reproduced from Broadband Finder

Figure 5.5

6. Print the details of the package you want, or write them down.

    You'll want these details for later reference and any further comparisons you decide to do.

7. If you want to proceed to order, click the Proceed to Checkout button and complete the order.

Again, I recommend that you give yourself a 'cooling off' period before making a decision. Also, you should consider a mobile broadband plus laptop package before making a decision. I'll describe that in a later section.

> Now that you've used Broadband Finder, you can click the Home link and use the Compare Broadband area to search for home broadband as well. I'll also recommend that you return to Broadband Finder if you want to look for a mobile broadband plus laptop package in the next section.

Installing home broadband

Home broadband providers like to have you set up your own home broadband, something most of us would prefer to avoid.

You can do it, though. The provider will send you detailed instructions. Here's an overview of the process to make you more comfortable about it:

- Begin by waiting. There's usually a wait for your phone line to be prepared and for the needed equipment to be sent out to you. Your provider will let you know when to expect the line to be ready and the equipment to arrive.

- The provider sends you a router, cables and a set-up disk. The router is a little grey box about the size of a paperback book with several lights on it. It converts a signal from a phone line into a wireless radio signal that permeates your house. (If you're lucky, it will permeate your whole house, not just parts of it.)

- You use included cables to connect the router to your phone line. The core of the process is a 'splitter', a little piece of cable with two heads that allows you to plug both your phone and your router into the same phone plug in the wall. If your phone cable is hard-wired into the wall, you'll need to arrange for an engineer to come to your home to upgrade your phone line.

- Once the router is plugged into the phone line, you also plug it into power and turn it on. It should then fill the air with a wireless Internet radio signal. This is your personal home broadband network.

- You put the set-up CD that comes with the router in your laptop. The set-up CD runs and installs any needed software on your laptop. (These days, a new laptop should already have the needed software on it, but you can never be sure.)

- You should now be able to detect the wireless Internet signal from your laptop, as described in the next chapter.

- On your laptop, choose your new wireless broadband network. You may now have to enter a long, obscure 26-character code that comes with your router. It's usually prominently marked on the router's accompanying documentation. You should only have to do this once, but keep the code handy in case someone else wants to log into your router.

You should have broadband wireless Internet access in your home from then on.

If you feel nervous about this process, you can get help. You may have friends or family members who have been through it before and can help, or ask your Guardian Angel. Alternatively, your broadband provider may offer to have an installer come out, though this will usually cost you money. I recommend that you try it yourself, or with the help of a friend or family member, first.

Buying your laptop in a package deal

There's a new option for buying a laptop that's just become viable in the last few years, one which you should consider.

This option is buying your laptop as a package deal which includes mobile broadband. Packages which include home broadband are now quite rare, but bundles with mobile broadband are common.

There were package deals for laptops that included home broadband, but these may no longer be available. Carphone Warehouse, which bought the UK rights to the AOL service, might be a good place to check on this if you're interested. It's worth investigating all your options before making a final decision.

Mobile broadband packages with a laptop are very similar to mobile phone deals where you get a free or discounted mobile phone in exchange for staying on a mobile service contract for 12 months, 18 months or 24 months.

Most of the 'laptops' offered on bundle deals are really netbooks or other very small computers. Insist on a full-sized laptop with a 14-inch or 15-inch screen and all the other features you want.

It seems kind of odd for a whole laptop to just be 'tossed in' along with the price of your Internet connection, but these offers can be a good option if you manage them correctly. Here's how this works:

- You may pay extra, two to three times the normal monthly broadband charge, to pay for the 'free' laptop.

- The laptop cost built into the price is not that high, because the provider can get laptops a lot cheaper than an individual customer can.

- During the contract, you're winning – you get a good price on the laptop and the equivalent of no-interest monthly payments.

- At the end of the contract, if you immediately switch to a normal, cheaper broadband charge, you win. If you keep paying the extra, higher charge after the contract period, you're paying too much, and you lose.

Let's do the maths. A low-cost laptop plus mobile broadband deal at the time of writing is £25 a month on a 24 month contract. This is for an HP laptop with a 15-inch screen. The total cost to you during the contract is £600. Wireless broadband during this same period would cost you £10 a month, or £240 over 24 months. So the cost of the laptop to you is £360, less than you would have paid otherwise, and split into convenient monthly payments as well.

However, every month you stay on the higher tariff after the contract is over makes the laptop – by now old and probably a bit clapped out – £20 more expensive, so be sure to switch away as soon as the 24 month contract period is up.

Package deals can be bad deals if you stay on the higher tariff after the contract term is over. Make sure to create plenty of reminders to yourself to switch when the time comes.

To shop for a laptop with mobile broadband, visit providers who offer these deals. There are three main types:

1. Mobile phone shops that offer various providers – in the UK, this includes Carphone Warehouse, Phones 4U and The Link.

2. PC vendors also offer these deals, in combination with a mobile phone shop or on their own. To name a few in the UK: PC World, Curry's, Dixons and many others.

3. The main mobile phone service providers in the UK, 3, O2, Orange, T-Mobile and Virgin, may also offer them.

Reproduced by permission of © DSG international plc

Figure 5.6

Look carefully at the laptops on offer. It's not worth getting a laptop you wouldn't want just because it's inexpensive. Find a laptop you would have been happy to buy as a standalone offering.

You may get the widest choice by shopping for your PC from a traditional PC vendor, as described in the previous chapter, then considering mobile broadband as an add-on.

Buying a laptop deal or package deal online is not usually a good idea, as you could be disappointed by the actual laptop that gets shipped to you. (Shopping online is a good idea; buying often isn't, if you don't see the product first.) Visit the shops in person to find a laptop you really like. Then use an online search, if you have access, to find reviews and prices for the laptop you're considering purchasing in a package deal.

Summary

● Broadband access is crucial to getting the most out of your laptop.

● You can get home broadband to share with all the PCs at home, mobile broadband for when you're on the move, or both.

● You can also buy a PC as a package deal with mobile broadband, but this is only worthwhile for most people if the mobile broadband service also covers your home broadband needs.

● There are useful online services for shopping for home broadband and for mobile broadband, and both are also offered in many PC and mobile phone shops.

● Shop around. Look online and in stores before making your decision, so you are aware of all the options available to you.

Brain Training

There may be more than one correct answer to these questions.

1. How long do you have to wait for home broadband to be switched on?

a) No wait at all

b) Up to 24 hours

c) Up to 48 hours

d) One to two weeks

2. How long do you have to wait for mobile broadband to start working?

a) No wait at all

b) Up to 24 hours

c) Up to 48 hours

d) One to two weeks

3. Which offers more data transfer capacity in a basic package?

a) Home broadband

b) Mobile broadband

c) Satellite navigation

d) Dial-up

4. What kind of package deal is commonly available?

a) Home broadband and a laptop

b) Mobile broadband and a laptop

c) Home broadband and phone service

d) Home broadband, phone and TV service

5. Who should use mobile broadband as their only broadband?

a) Anyone

b) Light users with good mobile signal strength at home

c) Heavy users with lots of computers in the home

d) No one

Answers

Q1 – d   **Q2** – a   **Q3** – a   **Q4** – b, c and d

Q5 – b

Bringing your laptop home

6

Equipment needed: Your new laptop; broadband access.
Optional: peripherals such as a printer.

Skills needed: Basic knowledge of the keyboard, mouse and
operating system to be able to test your laptop's functionality
and ensure everything works.

Identifying the laptop you want and buying it, as described in the previous
chapters, can be really exciting. But it's even more exciting to get the laptop
home, along with all the 'bits and pieces' that go with it.

I suggest you contact your insurance company soon after purchasing your
laptop to ensure it is covered. Take the opportunity to get specific details on
exactly what's covered and what isn't. Your insurance company may ask for
the serial number, purchase price and so on. Providing this information may
speed things up if you ever have to make a claim. (Something you hopefully
will never have to do, but it's best to be covered).

Set aside plenty of space for the laptop, and any other equipment such as a
printer, during setup. You may want to take over the kitchen table or some other
area for a while so you can see all the 'bits and pieces' that go with setup. You can
then move everything to its long-term home when you're done.

In this chapter I'll take you through the details, what you need to keep and what you can safely throw away. At the end of it you should have your laptop up and running and be sure that everything is working as it should.

> If you can arrange to have a knowledgeable friend, family member or your guardian angel with you, it's a good time to get a bit of help. Make sure that it's someone who's willing to take their time with you. Setting up your laptop is a great chance to learn more about how it works.

Setting your laptop up at home

Using your laptop safely at home takes a bit of thought, but it is very important.

> If you intend to use your laptop for a long period, it is important that you are sitting comfortably. Take plenty of breaks and don't sit in the same position for too long. I suggest you sit in a comfortable chair with some padding to it and with room for your knees, so you aren't leaning too far forward to type.

You also need a good working space and to know what to keep out of all the packaging that comes with your laptop. I'll explain that too.

Setting your laptop up correctly

Experts on ergonomics prefer that the screen you use be just below the level of your eyes. This is difficult with a laptop, where the screen is joined by a hinge to the keyboard and can't be independently raised. If you find that, after looking down for a period, you have problems in your back, neck or shoulders, consider buying an external monitor that you can raise to eye level for comfort.

Another possible technique is to buy an external keyboard and mouse and raise the laptop itself on phone books or reams of copier paper.

My three top tips for using a laptop safely are:

- **Learning to type properly**. If you never learned to type, now might be a good time to learn, as typing properly can also mean typing painlessly. Consider buying a typing program; I found some useful results by searching on 'learning to type properly' at **www.google.co.uk**.

Reproduced by permission of Google™ © 2009

Figure 6.1

- **Typing with your wrists in the air**. The natural tendency when using a laptop is to rest your wrists on the front edge of the computer, then hold your fingers in a claw position to type. This strains your fingers. A better way to do it is for your hands to be in the air and only your fingers touching the computer. This feels like extra work, but is less stressful on the wrists for sustained use. To do this, your chair needs to be fairly high relative to your laptop (your laptop, that is).

- **Not overusing a mouse**. I overused computers for several weeks in a row about twenty years ago and ended up with a very sore right wrist. It turns out that this was from a combination of typing and using a mouse. I switched to using a mouse left-handed and now have no problems, but if I use a mouse right-handed for even a few minutes, the pain returns.

Here are two resources for learning to type better. The first is an article on the Web that lists several useful learn-to-type sites:

http://mashable.com/2008/01/02/learn-how-to-type-faster-with-these-8-sites/

Reproduced by permission of Mashable.com

Figure 6.2

The other is a free program you can download from one of the best sites around, download.com. Visit **www.download.com** and search for 'typing master', in quotes. The program is free to try and is currently about £30 to buy.

Instructions for safely setting up and using a laptop in your home should come with your laptop. You can find additional information online. Here's one useful site that sums up key information in just a few pages:

http://www.cdha.nshealth.ca/default.aspx?page=DocumentRender&doc
.Id=2838

Reproduced by permission of Capital District Health Authority, Halifax, Nova Scotia, Canada

Figure 6.3

This site includes helpful tips and advice for maintaining good posture when using either a laptop or a desktop computer.

Finding space at home

Now that you know what it takes to use a laptop safely, you can see that it requires more than an area just for the laptop, but also everything that goes with it. Here's what you need to accommodate everything:

● **Plenty of space**. You need enough desktop space for the computer itself, a mouse and mouse pad (if you decide to buy a mouse for your laptop)

● **Room for your printer**. You need a good home for the printer, hopefully near the computer. You may need access to the top of the printer, for scanning or making copies, and room for the documents tray in front or on the side. You can have a socket connected or a wireless printer a good distance from your computer. However, it can be better to have it nearby so you can quickly check that it's doing what you want, deal with paper jams etc.

- **Safe plug access**. Once you know where you want to keep your laptop, make sure you have easy access to sockets. Don't stretch cables too tightly or place extension lead sockets too close to curtains or furniture. Keep cable leads against walls where possible, to avoid potential trip hazards.

- **Easy unplugging access**. You may find yourself frequently unplugging your laptop and taking the laptop and its electrical cord elsewhere in the house, or out and about with you. Bear this in mind when choosing the location of your laptop.

- **Good light.** You need soft light – coming from behind you. Avoid the strong glare of sunlight and certainly do not work with no light at all. Working by the light from your laptop alone can strain your eyes trying to see the keyboard. (A few computers have a keyboard that lights up gently in the dark, but most don't.)

Despite the fact that a laptop is flexible, you need a good workspace for sustained use of a laptop. Don't fall into the habit of getting by with setting it on the kitchen table, or your lap, every time you want to use it. It is sometimes a good idea to use a proper desk and chair, where possible. There are special desks for computer use at office supply stores and in furniture shops, including affordable ones such as Ikea.

British sockets can be turned on and off at the source; once your laptop is shut down correctly, it is a good idea to turn off the socket for your laptop. This protects it from power surges that may come during a storm, for instance.

Also, if you look at your laptop cord, you'll see it has a cheaper part, with the three-pronged plug for the wall on it, and an expensive part, with the actual power converter and the plug that goes into the laptop itself. The two parts usually plug into one another and can be detached. Consider getting an extra copy of the cheaper part to take with you, so you can leave the original cheaper part plugged in when you move around. (With the plug turned off at the source, of course.) I've found this makes dealing with the power cord much easier.

Unpacking the laptop

After removing the laptop from the box, I suggest you keep the original packaging and everything in it for some time. If you decide to return the laptop, the store will want it with its original packaging. The laptop may also come with a recovery disk, for use in solving serious problems; a manual; phone numbers for support; and other bits and bobs that could be important. So don't throw things out right away.

Be especially careful to keep any CD-ROM disks and DVDs that come with the laptop or with software you buy. These are invaluable if you need to restore your system after a problem.

Once the laptop is out of the box, you have five important tasks, and the one that may seem the most important is actually the least urgent. You probably want to learn how your laptop works and start using it right away. However, I suggest the order of your priorities should be:

1. Ensuring everything works.
2. Getting rid of unnecessary software (bloatware).
3. Adding new software, as appropriate.
4. Making sure everything works (again).
5. Trying your laptop to learn how it works.

Here's how to perform each of these steps in turn. I'll cover all of them in this chapter except for the last one. I'll touch on point 5 throughout this chapter, then explore it in more depth throughout the remainder of the book.

Making sure everything works

Ensuring everything is in working order is a priority because you'll want to find out as soon as possible if there are any problems or faults that suggest you may need to return your laptop to the vendor. In this chapter I'll take you through testing the most important aspects of the system. Of course, in doing this checking, you'll learn quite a bit about how your laptop works as well.

When you first get your laptop home, take it out of the box carefully. You'll get used to handling it over time, but at first it might be an awkward object to handle, so be careful.

If you've purchased a mouse, plug it in. Most mice today are USB mice; plug this into one of your USB ports. Once you switch on the laptop, the mouse should be recognised by the system and the software supporting it will generally be installed automatically. If not, check the instruction manual which came with the mouse.

Plug the laptop in and switch it on. (When new, the battery will be low from being in the box, so use your laptop from the mains to begin with.) You'll see it start up, which will take a minute or so. Even after the Windows or Mac desktop appears, you'll still need to wait, as the computer is still working.

Once the system is fully started, go through the following checks to make sure everything is working properly.

Screen test

Sorry, the 'screen test' isn't your chance to star in Hollywood! It's just a careful check of your laptop's screen to make sure it's in good shape. The screen is one of the indispensable parts of a laptop and can't generally be replaced without replacing the entire machine. So inspecting it is a good first step in protecting yourself.

You need to inspect the screen soon after taking the laptop out of its box to check it is not damaged. The screen test will also ensure that basic software functionality is in place and will begin familiarising you with your laptop.

These first few steps can be tedious but don't worry; things that seem painstakingly detailed at first become second nature after a few tries. To begin with I will give comprehensive, step-by-step instructions but as you become more confident I will go into less detail.

The specific instructions given here are for Windows. If you have a Mac, please modify the steps slightly as appropriate.

1. Inspect the desktop. Particularly note the Taskbar, a large strip at the bottom of the screen that shows you what programs are open and displays important information about the system, such as the time, wireless network access and remaining battery power.

   I have my Taskbar set up to give me one-click access to my most frequently used programs and to display the information I care about most; remaining battery power, wireless access status and the date and time. I also have it stretched to double the minimum width to allow me to see more description when I have half a dozen or so windows open at once. You can customise the taskbar to meet your individual needs.

2. Move your mouse to the Start button, the large round button in the lower left corner of the screen, as shown in Figure 6.4.

   The Start menu only says Start when you hold the mouse over it without clicking. This is called 'hovering' the mouse or 'mousing over' the button. The text is called 'mouseover text'. (Think of a mouse scampering over a newspaper on the floor. Mouse over text!)

3. Click the Start button. The Start menu appears.

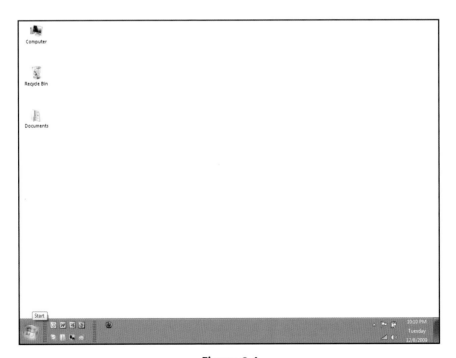

Figure 6.4

The Start menu shows a number of programs prominently. You can change these programs.

4. Mouse over the All Programs line.

    After a moment, a list of programs will appear. Individual programs with colourful icons appear at the top, in alphabetical older, followed by identical folder icons, also in alphabetical order. Some programs are in folders and some aren't, though not for any useful reason.

5. Click the scrolling button in the right hand side of the list and drag it to make the list of programs scroll. Find the Accessories folder (after the individual programs and at the top of the list of folders).

    This display of programs can be a bit overwhelming at first, but after a few tries you'll be whizzing through it like a pro.

6. Click the Accessories folder once.

    A list of utility programs available on every Windows machine opens, as shown in Figure 6.5. It's like a toolbox with basics like a screwdriver, hammer and so on.

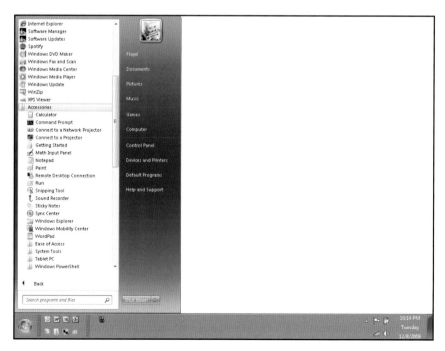

Figure 6.5

7. Move the mouse down to the Notepad icon and click.

Notepad, a bare-bones word processing tool with very few features, will open. A button showing the open Notepad window appears in the taskbar.

We could also have used Wordpad, a basic word processing program also available in Accessories, but Notepad presents a lot more white area onscreen, which is what we need for this test.

In the upper right corner of the Notepad window, you'll see three controls – a squat little box, a larger, open box, and an X. These controls are available on just about every Windows program window.

Figure 6.6

The squat little box minimises the window – reduces it to a button in your list of open programs. The larger, open box maximises the window – makes it fill the entire screen area. The X closes the window and, in some cases, the entire program that has the window open. (If you have any unsaved data in the window, you'll be asked to save it before the program closes.)

8. Click the middle control in the upper right corner of the Notepad window – the larger, open box.

The Notepad window will enlarge to occupy the entire screen.

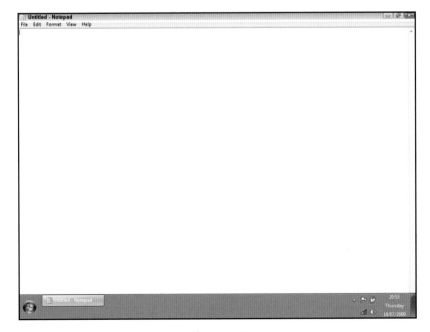

Figure 6.7

9. Right-click on an empty part of the Taskbar.

   A menu will appear.

10. Click Properties, the lowest option on the menu.

    The Taskbar and Start Menu Properties dialogue will appear. (A 'dialogue' is a window that asks you for information to use in managing a program or a task you're carrying out.)

11. In the Taskbar and Start Menu Properties dialogue, click the checkbox, Auto-hide the taskbar.

    The box will show a tick mark.

12. Still in the Taskbar and Start Menu Properties dialogue, click Apply.

    The taskbar will disappear! It will re-appear anytime you pause the mouse over the area it occupies. Try hovering the mouse over the area to see the taskbar re-appear.

    Since you previously chose Maximise for the Notepad, the Notepad window will expand to fill the empty space.

13. In the Taskbar and Start Menu Properties dialogue, click OK.

    The OK button means 'Go away, dialogue, I'm done'.

14. Now for the fun part: carefully inspect the screen for any black spots. These are called 'dead pixels'. Also look for pixels that aren't fully white.

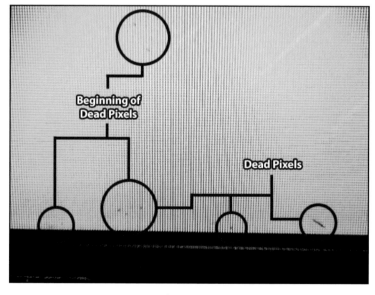

Figure 6.8

Each pixel is quite small, about 1/72 inch to 1/100 inch. You probably won't see individual dead pixels without a magnifying glass, as they're so small. You don't need to look that closely; you're looking for easily visible problems that will make your laptop less useful.

If you do see visible problems, sufficient to bother you, return the laptop and ask for a replacement.

Note that a few small areas along the top of the laptop screen are either black text (in the upper left) or program controls (in the upper right). You can inspect those too.

Don't be put off if you find just a few dead pixels on very close inspection. Manufacturing laptop screens is quite tricky, and a few dead pixels are considered acceptable. Just identify if there are easily visible dead or discoloured areas big enough to bother you in normal use.

15. If you look closely at the Notepad window, you'll see the middle control in the upper right area has changed. Hover the mouse over it to see its name; the button is called 'restore down'. Click 'restore down' to return the Notepad window to its former size. Move the window around on the screen so you can inspect the areas that were occupied by black text or icons before.

    You've thoroughly checked your screen now.

16. Once you're finished inspecting the screen, restore things to the original state: Click the X button to close the window. Hover the mouse over the taskbar area to make it appear, and right-click. Choose Properties from the menu that appears and unclick the checkbox, Auto-Hide the Taskbar. Click OK.

    It will probably already be starting to feel natural to open and close windows and change settings.

    Congratulations! You've completed your first task on your new laptop. You've not only ensured that your screen is in good working order, but also got a feel for opening and closing programs, using dialogue boxes, managing the Taskbar and managing program windows.

    In the remaining tests, I'll give more abbreviated steps so as to reflect what you've already learned.

The checks given here are only for checking your laptop's functionality and only go a small part of the way to getting you familiar with Windows or the Mac. For more information on these important topics, consider *Computing for the Older and Wiser* (ISBN 9780470770993), *Computing with Windows 7 for the Older and Wiser* (ISBN 9780470687031) or *Mac for Dummies* (ISBN 9780470278178). You can use the ISBN number as a reference to find these books in a library, bookstore or online store.

Keyboard, trackpad and mouse tests

During the first day or two after you purchase a laptop, the vendor may accept a return for almost any reason (check this before buying, as some stores have different return policies). After that, however, it gets progressively more difficult to justify, as well as to prove that you didn't cause the problem yourself. (The first question they'll ask you if you try to return it later is, 'Why didn't you return it right away?'). So check the computer thoroughly as soon as you get it home to make sure it functions as it's supposed to. Always keep the receipt as proof of purchase.

I'll now run through some steps to check the other important functions of your laptop. Your goal is to make sure that it's fit for use.

Once you're sure the screen is acceptable, it's time to check the keyboard, trackpad and mouse. Follow these steps:

1. Open Notepad, as in the previous set of steps.

    The steps to open a program are often given in an abbreviated form, like this: Start ➪ All Programs ➪ Accessories ➪ Notepad. This means: 'Click Start; choose All Programs; choose Accessories; choose Notepad'.

2. Type a few sentences into Notepad. Be sure to use every key on the keyboard. Check that all the keys are responsive and none are sticky, dead or loose. A single sticky or 'dead' key can drive you nuts, whereas a fully responsive keyboard is a joy to use.

Type a varied sentence like 'The quick brown fox jumped over the lazy red dogs' to check all the keys. Then type every key in turn, including number and symbol keys. A loose or sticky key on your keyboard is like a loose tooth – it wouldn't bother you much if you could ignore it, but you can't, so it will drive you crazy. Check carefully for bad keys and get the keys, or the computer itself, fixed or replaced if you find any.

3. Select a sentence using the mouse: move the cursor to the start of the sentence, then drag to select the sentence and release the cursor. Repeat with the trackpad.

   The text will be highlighted to show it's selected. Trying this with both the mouse and trackpad will give you a feel for which is more comfortable for you.

If the mouse hesitates, you may need a new mouse mat or a new mouse. Wireless mice in particular can be hesitant and jumpy, particularly if they are out of range of their connecting port on the computer. If you have a wireless mouse that feels jumpy, you may want to consider replacing the wireless mouse with a wired one.

4. Copy the selected text: hold down the Control key (usually labelled ctrl), press C and release it, then release the Control key. This is typically shown in instructions as Ctrl+C. Then move the cursor to a new location and paste the text (Ctrl+V). Also try dragging the selected text to a new location.

5. Repeat selecting and moving text with the mouse and trackpad for a few minutes. Also, after you enter several chunks of text, test keys such as Page Up and Page Down.

   Make sure the keyboard, mouse and trackpad are all working smoothly for you.

6. Try special function keys and other hardware controls.

   Your laptop may have special keyboard controls and other keys for screen brightness, volume and other functions. Test the keys that you can now. When you later test other functionality such as playing a DVD, test the volume controls.

As you use the keyboard, trackpad and mouse, make sure your hands, wrists, arms, neck, shoulders and back are all comfortable. Take a break often to let your tendons and muscles get used to the new kind of work.

Battery test

One of the most important features to test on your new laptop is the battery life. There are three good reasons for testing this early on:

- **If it's broken, they have to fix it**. Battery life claims can heavily sway a consumer's decision when buying a laptop. If your laptop doesn't live up to the manufacturer's claims – and many don't – you need to consider a replacement laptop or even a different model.

- **Know before you go**. It's important to know what you can expect before you use your laptop on the move. Should you bring along that power cord or not? The answer depends on how long the laptop will run whilst unplugged.

- **Keep it fresh**. Many laptop batteries keep capacity better if they're periodically allowed to discharge completely, then fully recharged. So it's a good idea to run your laptop battery down all the way once every week or two then recharge it.

Checking battery life is simple:

1. Give your laptop time to charge fully.

   This should take just a few hours, even if it was fully discharged before.

2. Check to make sure the battery is fully charged by hovering the mouse cursor over the battery icon in the System Notification area to the right of the Taskbar. It should say Fully charged (100%).

   There should be an icon showing the current battery level and whether the computer is plugged in. If not, right-click in the taskbar and choose Properties from the cursor menu that appears. Click the link, 'How do I customise the taskbar?', to learn how to display the current battery level in the taskbar.

3. Unplug your laptop from the power plug, or turn off the power plug at the wall.

4. Use your laptop until the battery runs out.

   Note how long you actively use the laptop versus how long it's just sitting idle.

   You should get several warnings when your battery is running low. Save any work you have in progress, but otherwise ignore them. Eventually, your computer will go into hibernation – a kind of 'sleep' – or actually run out of power.

5. Plug your computer back in.

   Note how many hours and minutes of active use you got before the computer shut down.

   If the useful time is considerably less than advertised, consider returning the laptop. Any laptop sold today should be able to provide at least two hours of active use running from the battery, and preferably three or more.

   If the useful time is satisfactory, you can keep the system. Keep the usage time in mind for future excursions with your laptop.

If you need to return your laptop, the way you describe problems can help you get a refund. For instance, if you say, 'I didn't like the keyboard', you may have a hard time. If you say, 'The keyboard didn't perform the way I expected it to', which is just as true, your refund might come more easily.

Wireless test

Now for one of the most important test of all – making sure your laptop has wireless access. This one is probably easy for you to do, but it's hard to describe the process exactly because the circumstances for using wireless vary so much.

The ability of computers to pick up a wireless signal can vary significantly. It's hard to know just how able or not yours is unless it either works flawlessly or is pretty bad.

Some early Apple laptops had magnesium cases that did a remarkably good job of blocking wireless signals; these laptops were notably bad at connecting to wireless networks. Unless your laptop has a major problem like this, you'll probably never know exactly how it compares to other laptops' wireless capabilities.

So all you can test is whether your laptop works fairly well or not. Follow these steps to test:

1. Go somewhere that you know has a wireless network you can sign onto.

    If you have home broadband, this should work at home. If you have mobile broadband, it should work anywhere a mobile phone will work. If you don't have either of these set up yet, there should be a coffee shop, gym, pub, restaurant or hotel near you with wireless access for free, or at a low cost per hour. If you bought your computer in a shop, the shop should have a wireless network active that you can use for testing.

    You can also try using a wireless network at a friend's or family member's house, but you will need their wireless network sign-on code.

2. If your laptop has a wireless switch, make sure it is turned on.

    An off-off switch for wireless is a great thing to have on your laptop, because you can save a bit of battery life by turning wireless off when you don't need it. Sometimes, though, the switch is easy to turn off accidentally. Look for a switch of this kind (it may be well hidden) and make sure it's turned on.

3. Search for wireless networks. Click on the taskbar icon that shows a series of bars or choose Start ⇨ Control Panel ⇨ Network and Internet ⇨ View network status and tasks.

    The dialogue, View your basic network information and set up connections, appears.

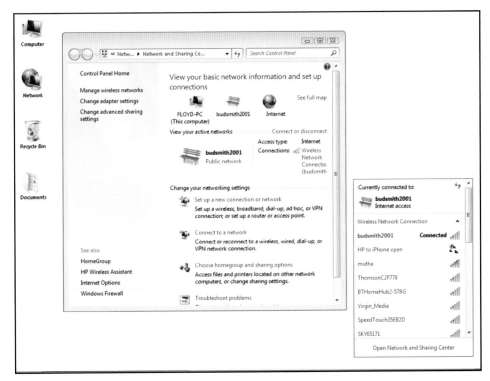

Figure 6.9

4. Click Connect to a network.

    If there are no wireless networks present, or if your wireless access is turned off or broken, you'll see an error message. If there are wireless networks present, you'll see a list of available networks.

5. From the list of available networks, choose the one you're trying to log onto.

    You may be surprised to see a lot of wireless networks nearby. Choose yours from the list.

6. Click the wireless network you want.

    It should connect to the network. However, even if you're connected, you may not have full access yet. Check the next step.

7. Open a web browser such as Internet Explorer; click Start ⇨ All Programs ⇨ Internet Explorer.

Internet Explorer will open. If you're in a location that requires sign-on, such as a coffee shop, you'll be asked for a code – usually a separate user name and password – to proceed. Ask staff at the location for this information.

8. Enter the user name and password, if required, and click OK, Login or similar button.

The Internet Explorer window should open a different site.

9. Go to a site of your choice, such as **www.wiley.com**, by entering its web address in the strip at the top of the screen.

The website should open.

If you can see a screen similar to the image below congratulation it worked! You have working wireless network functionality on your laptop.

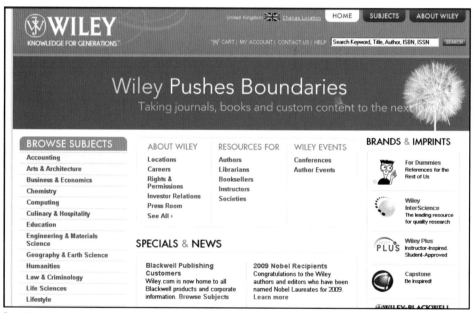

Reproduced with permission of Wiley & Sons, Ltd.

Figure 6.10

If not, try asking a friend or your guardian angel for advice. Or go back to the shop where you got the computer to ask their advice. (Alternatively phone the help line number, if you bought the laptop online.) Try to get help with either fixing the problem or returning the computer if it is a more serious fault.

Additional functionality test

The screen, keyboard, trackpad and mouse, battery and wireless access checks all test and confirm the functionality of the most important parts of your computer that are likely to have problems. If you like, you can check additional functionality:

● **DVD.** Try playing a DVD. Make sure the visual quality and sound quality are acceptable. You should hear sound from speakers on both sides – make sure neither is broken. See if the screen keeps up during fast-moving parts of the action. Test any keys your laptop has for volume and for brightness control. Check the viewing angle – to what extent can you watch from an angle to the screen?

● **Headset**. If you own a headset, playing a DVD is a good time to test the headphone jack (socket). To test the microphone, check the instructions that come with the system, or try a Skype phone call at **www.skype.com**.

● **Bluetooth support**. If you have Bluetooth support and any Bluetooth devices, see if you can get them to communicate with your computer.

● **Web cam.** If you have a built-in or add-on web cam, it should come with instructions on how to test it. If you don't have any, try a video call on Skype at **www.skype.com**.

● **Virus protection**. Open your virus protection program and have it do a full system scan. The scan may take a long time, but you should be able to continue working while it runs in the background.

● **Printer**. Connect up your printer and make sure you can print a page. Find a web page with pictures on it – Flickr, at **www.flickr.com**, is one such site – and print a page or two to test your printer's functionality and print quality.

● **USB drive** ('thumb drive'). Plug in your USB drive and copy a file or two to it, then back again.

Check that everything works. You need to be sure on the first day or two of owning your laptop. After that, the old saying, 'you broke it, you own it' will begin to apply.

Deleting software

Scientists like to say that something that doesn't feel natural is 'counterintuitive'. I'm about to recommend a 'counterintuitive' step in setting up your laptop: once you've made sure everything works, delete unnecessary software.

This may give rise to two questions: Why? And why now?

The reason for getting rid of unnecessary software is that it clogs up your system. It can make the start-up run slower and also uses precious RAM. Having software in RAM that doesn't need to be there can make the system slower in general. (The programs also take up hard disk space, but usually not enough to cause problems.) This so-called bloatware can also cause problems like odd error messages that appear for no known reason.

Many applications that are pre-loaded on new laptops are trial versions. They persistently pester you to buy the full version. For instance, an anti-virus program might warn you that 'protection is about to expire', even if you've already purchased and installed a different anti-virus program.

It is important to be aware that deleting a program could simultaneously delete an underlying support file that other applications need in order to run. This in turn can lead the system to become unstable. If this happens, the only remedy is to re-install the computer's operating software. This can be a confusing process, and if in doubt I would advise you to seek the help of your guardian angel.

Deleting bloatware is much easier to do at the beginning, which is where the 'why now?' comes in. Should you inadvertently delete a vital system file, requiring the reinstalling of system files, any data you have previously saved to your laptop will be lost.

This kind of problem happens rarely, but doing your cleanup before you install other applications reduces the potential for problems further on. Plus, it's better to be safe than sorry.

Sometimes trial software is less well-known software, not the premium brands that people usually buy. You're usually better off with the top brands as they're better-supported, more people know how to use them and can help you, there are more books, videos and websites about how to use them, and so on.

You may have to work with your laptop for a while for all of these trial versions to appear, as some of them appear at startup and others at various intervals. Once you've determined what trialware you wish to uninstall, here's how to delete trial applications:

1. Click Start ⇨ Control Panel.

   The Windows Control Panel will appear.

2. Click Programs ⇨ Uninstall a Program.

   A list of programs will appear.

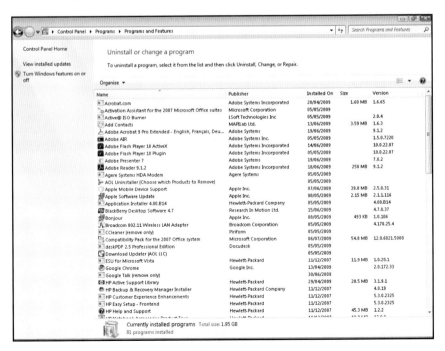

Figure 6.11

3. Use the scrolling list to find the application you want to delete. Click the application, then click the Uninstall link at the top of the window.

   A dialogue will appear asking you to confirm that you want to delete the program.

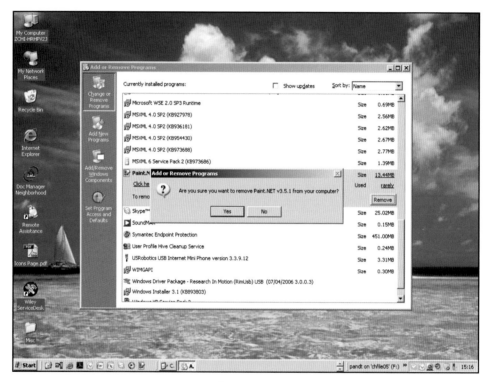

Figure 6.12

4. Click Yes.

   The program will be removed.

5. Repeat steps 3 and 4 for all the programs you want to remove.

   Your computer may become less stable after you delete applications until you restart.

6. Restart your computer.

   Windows will restart.

7. Try opening an application and visiting a website just to make sure everything still works.

This process will remove some but not all of the bloatware on your system. It takes an expert to really get rid of all traces of bloatware.

Loading software

Once you've deleted some or all of the programs that have been bothering you, it's time to load new software. Some laptops come with trial or even full software on a CD-ROM or DVD in the box. It may be pre-installed or it may not.

You may also have purchased software with your system. Now is the time to load it. Open the package and follow the instructions for each program. Usually, if you simply insert the CD-ROM or DVD for the program in your new laptop's DVD drive, the installation program will start automatically.

If you accept the pre-selected installation options, you'll usually get what you need. (If you later need a feature that didn't load as part of the normal installation, such as foreign language support, the program will ask you to re-insert the installation disk and will load the feature for you. So keep your installation disks!)

In addition to software that comes with your laptop or that you purchase, there's Web-based software that you need to have, and that you want the latest versions of. Your laptop may already have some of this software, but this might easily be a year old. So even if you have the needed program, you may not have the latest version.

Sometimes web-based software is shown as being in a beta version. This means the software is not quite complete. For name brand software, at least, you can usually use the beta version in the knowledge that it won't cause serious problems, though it may cause you to need to restart your system more often than non-beta software. Save your open files early and often.

With the most-needed software at the top, here's my list and where to go to get it:

Early versions of Internet Explorer were jokingly called 'Internet Exploder' because they were unstable and prone to errors.

● **Internet Explorer** is now the most popular Internet browser by far, and the one that works with the most websites. Due to antitrust agreements, it isn't included on new PCs shipped in Europe. You can get the latest version at **www.microsoft.com/ie**.

● **Adobe® Reader®**. Adobe controls the PDF, which stands for Portable Document Format, standard. PDF files retain the original formatting of the document they were created from and usually print as a more or less exact duplicate of the original. You will find many PDF files on the Web, and you need Adobe Reader to view and print them. Visit **www.adobe.com/reader** for the latest version. Be sure to unclick the option for the free Google Toolbar unless you really want it (see below).

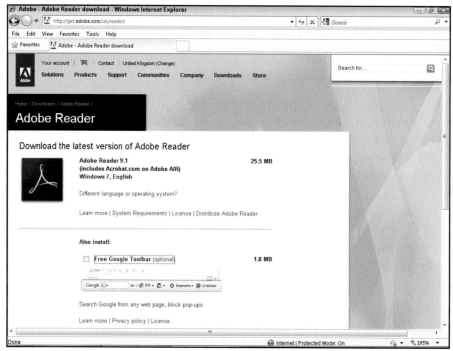

Adobe product screenshot reproduced from Adobe Systems Incorporated.

Figure 6.13

- **Adobe® Flash®.** Flash is a multimedia add-on for web pages. It's quite controversial because it can have a different 'look and feel' than the rest of the Web. However, it's sometimes used simply to make video clips play better on web sites; the very popular YouTube video site uses Flash for this purpose. Visit **www.adobe.com/flash** for the latest version of Flash.

- **Apple QuickTime.** Apple QuickTime is mildly popular for movie playback on the Web. You'll definitely need it if you play movie clips on the Apple website, which hosts some very nice ones. Find QuickTime at **www.apple. com/quicktime**.

- **Apple iTunes.** iTunes is the most popular software for legally downloading songs over the Internet. iTunes songs, at the time of writing, nearly all cost 79p each. iTunes is worthwhile just to get songs to play on your computer and invaluable if you have a portable digital music player, especially an iPod. You also need iTunes if you have an iPhone and want to buy applications for it in the famous App Store. You can get iTunes at **www.apple.com/itunes**.

- **Google Toolbar.** The Google Toolbar makes Google search always available from your Web browser. It also supports advanced features such as searching within a site and automatic translation of pages. However, newer browser versions can be set up to automatically search using Google, though without the special features. The need for Google Toolbar has therefore decreased. If you want Google Toolbar, you can find it at **www.google.com/toolbar**.

Summary

- Creating a comfortable place where you can plug in and use your laptop is good for your comfort and also your health.

- Using your laptop for long periods of time can naturally cause some aches and pains. Don't forget to take regular breaks!

- Getting rid of unneeded software can be just as important as loading up all the programs you really need. But be cautious when deleting software.

- A laptop should give you about three hours of battery life.

Brain Training

There may be more than one correct answer to these questions.

1. Why is it important to type properly on a laptop?

a) To get things done quickly

b) To win online typing speed competitions

c) To reduce the odds of being injured

d) So you look good while using your new laptop

2. Where should you put the printer?

a) Fairly near the laptop

b) On the other side of the room

c) In a different room entirely to cut out noise

d) It's best never to have a printer with a laptop

3. What's a good way to make space for a laptop desk?

a) Clear out items you no longer use

b) Remove kitchen appliances

c) Have extra people in the house move out

d) Remove bookcases or book shelving

4. What is unnecessary software on a laptop called?

a) Microsoft Office

b) Bloatware

c) Google

d) Accessories

5. What should you test as soon as you get your laptop home?

a) The screen is bright and undamaged

b) Wireless access works

c) All the keys on the keyboard work

d) Battery life is at least close to what was advertised

Answers

Q1 – a and c   **Q2** – a   **Q3** – a   **Q4** – b

Q5 – all answers

Customising the Windows desktop

Equipment needed: A laptop.

Skills needed: Basic knowledge of the keyboard, mouse and operating system.

Using a laptop can be very easy, when things are going well, but at times it can be frustrating if you don't fully understand all the laptop's functions. If you learn a little about how to use the software on your laptop, you can get more out of it and avoid problems.

Somewhat unfortunately, the software that manages what's on your laptop screen is 'configurable'. That means that the screen on two Windows 7 laptops can look quite different. If you use a laptop or desktop computer running an earlier version of Windows it can again look different. This can be confusing to begin with. It's like trying to drive a car where several of the controls are switched around.

For the Mac, the situation is now somewhat better. The Mac went through a big software and hardware transition about five years ago and is now quite stable, with each new release of software making relatively minor changes from the previous one. Moving from one to another is more like driving a newer model of the same kind of car.

Moving between Mac and Windows, though, is still quite difficult. When you move from one to the other, you naturally try to do the same things, but the results are often different. Sticking with our car analogy, this is akin to switching between a car with a manual and an automatic transmission. You're likely to miss a few gear shifts along the way!

In this chapter I'll take you through the major functions of using the 'desktop' of your new laptop, using Windows 7 as my specific example. This program is likely to come with new Windows computers. If you use a Mac, you can still follow along; the concepts are the same, but some of the specifics will be different.

The main functional difference for Mac is the lack of right-clicking, which is important in Windows. A Mac mouse typically has two buttons, but often is set to work as one. (You can change this, but can also often get the right-click effect by holding down the Control key, then clicking.) A Windows mouse or trackpad has two buttons.

The secret of setting up your laptop

The secret of configuring and using your laptop is to make using it as simple as possible. You don't want to have to think about what you're doing when you do your usual tasks. For instance, when you're about to go out for a walk, if you see nice weather, you leave your jumper or jacket at home. If it's about to rain, you grab an umbrella. Seeing the situation in front of you causes you to react automatically.

It's the same with your laptop. The programs and files that you use a lot should be right in front of you, so accessing them is automatic. In fact, a famous book about making products easy to use is called *Don't Make Me Think*. As you set up and use your laptop, arrange things so you don't have to think when you want to use them again and again.

Touring the desktop

The Mac and Windows desktops are meant to remind you of the top of a desk in the real world. It's a place you can put things you are using and get to tools that help you get your work done. In the real world, we all arrange our desks differently. Some of us leave them cluttered with 'bits and pieces' we use a lot – or a little. Others have a 'clean desk' policy and only have the bare minimum of what they're actually working on out on the desk at any one time. At the end of the day, everything is put away, ready for a fresh start the next day.

It's the same with the Windows desktop; you can use it in different ways depending on how you like to work. When you use someone else's computer, you have to deal with their idea of how to organise a desk, even if it's quite strange to your own way of working.

Let's look at what's on the desktop, and in the desk drawers, of a simple Windows desktop setup.

A clean desktop

A clean Windows desktop has just a few icons on the desktop – small images representing files, folders and programs – plus a strip called the Taskbar at the bottom. The Taskbar initially contains just the Start button and a few icons in what's called the Notification area, usually found in the lower right.

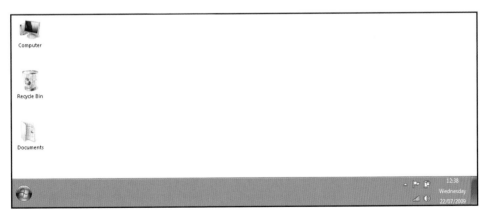

Figure 7.1

The icons on the desktop are of three types:

● **Icons Windows has put there**. It's best not to mess with these except by using Windows' Personalize capability, which I'll explain shortly.

- **Icons the system manufacturer has put there**. These may include valuable utilities and programs the manufacturer has provided, 'bloatware' that the manufacturer has put on in order to get paid by the provider, and programs somewhere between the two. You can almost always remove these from the desktop without much chance of problems.

Refer to Chapter 6 to see how to remove bloatware safely.

- **Icons you've put there** (perhaps without meaning to). You may have deliberately put files on the desktop. Also, as you install programs, the setup routine will often put an icon for that program on the desktop unless you make a specific choice for it not to. To keep your desktop as uncluttered as possible, you might want to keep these to a minimum.

You can make the Taskbar taller simply by dragging it. You can make it one, two or three icons high. The default setting from Microsoft is one icon high, but I routinely make mine two icons high so I can still read the task buttons when I'm running a lot of programs at once. You can also set the taskbar to auto-hide so it disappears until you hover the mouse over the lower edge of the screen; I rarely do this myself.

The Taskbar is also part of the desktop. It should only have a few things on it as well:

- **The Start button**. The Start button has a lot of functionality of its own, as I'll explain shortly. You can use it to start programs or to get to system settings or your documents.

- **The Notification area**. This should include at least five crucial notifications: power, wireless access, speaker volume, the Action Center and the icon for your virus protection program. It's also very convenient to have this area display the date and time.

- **The Show Desktop button**. A subtle bar off to the right edge of the Taskbar, the Show Desktop button clears all your screen windows (but not the Taskbar) and shows the desktop.

Desktop
button

Start
button

Notification area

Figure 7.2

For many users, the Taskbar is more important than the desktop itself. That's because the desktop is usually covered up by the open windows of various programs. Usually, only the Start menu and the Taskbar are accessible without going through the bothersome step of hiding all your running programs. So don't spend too much time on what's on the desktop; think more about the Start menu and the Taskbar.

The Windows menus, commands and help refer to the changes you can make to the system using different words – 'personalize' and 'customize' among them. I've used the word 'change' for consistency.

Changing the desktop background

A fun thing you can do in Windows is change the desktop background. I'll show you how to do this quickly and easily before getting into more detailed explanations of Windows functions.

The copy of Windows on your laptop almost certainly comes with images that are pre-selected to exactly fit the maximum resolution of the laptop's screen. If you use your own images, you can edit them to that resolution, or use one of the options described below to choose how the image will be handled onscreen.

Before you begin, if you have one or more pictures you want to use – for instance, pictures of friends or family members – you may want to move them temporarily to the Desktop or to the top level of your Documents folder. This will make it easy to find them and select them for your desktop background.

Windows makes it easy to choose multiple images, then put them into a rotation, so be ready to choose more than one image if you want to.

Now to change the background the simple way – to easily find and set one image as the desktop background:

1. Select your preferred image and save it to the desktop.

2. Right-click on the desktop.

   A context-sensitive menu appears.

3. Choose Personalize.

   The Personalization control panel appears.

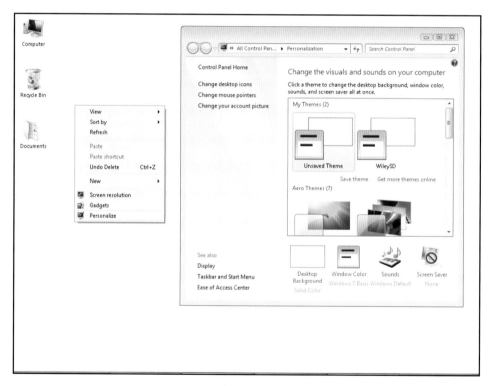

Figure 7.3

4. Click Desktop Background.

   The Desktop Background control panel appears.

5. Click Browse. Navigate to the Desktop and choose the picture you just put there.

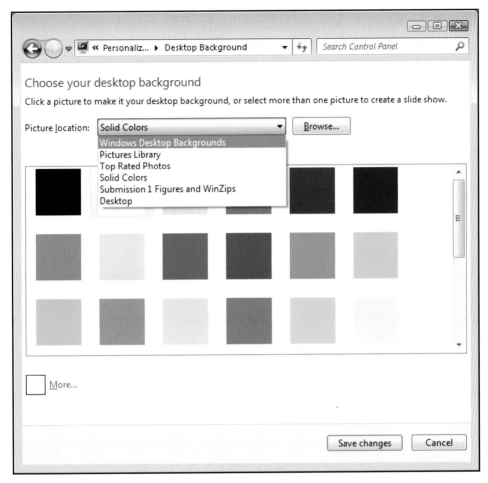

Figure 7.4

Any folder you choose while browsing will be added to the Picture Location drop-down menu and you can't get rid of it easily, so think twice before looking through a bunch of different folders.

6. To specify how the image is to be shown, choose Fill, Fit, Stretch, Tile or Center.

    Try different options; as you do, your desktop will be updated as a sort of live preview. Choose the option that looks best.

7. Click OK to set the chosen image and picture position as your desktop background.

That was the easy way, but you can make a lot more choices as well. Here's a detailed description of how to change the background, including all the options:

1. Right-click on the desktop.

    A context-sensitive menu appears.

2. Choose Personalize.

    The Personalization control panel appears.

3. Click Desktop Background.

    The Desktop Background control panel appears.

4. Rotate through the choices – Windows Desktop Backgrounds; Pictures Library; Top Rated Photos; Solid Colours. Click on different options.

    The desktop background will change temporarily to reflect each choice.

5. If you're experienced with using folders, click Browse. Navigate around your system to choose different picture files.

    You have to already know which folders contain images; Windows doesn't offer a preview.

    Don't forget any folder you choose while browsing will be added to the Picture Location drop-down menu and you can't easily get rid of it.

6. To choose an image, click it.

    If you click the image itself, any previous selection is un-clicked. If you click the check box in the upper corner, though, the image is added to previously selected images. The selected images stay selected until you un-tick the check box or click on the body of another image, making it the one and only selection. So remember where images are that you've clicked, as you'll have to find them again if you want to remove them from any rotation, or start again.

7. To choose a range of images, hold down the Shift key (to add all the images between one selection and the next one). Click a header such as Characters to choose all the images under that header. Use the Select All and Clear All buttons to choose or deselect a folder-full of images.

8. To change how pictures are handled, use the pull-down menu to choose Fill, Fit, Stretch, Tile or Center.

    These options can cause strange things to happen to your desktop image. Fill stretches the image proportionately to fit the desktop, cutting off any excess. Fit only stretches the image until it fills the desktop horizontally or vertically and inserts black bars to fill any gaps. Stretch stretches the image to fill the desktop completely, which can make people's faces, in particular, look quite weird. Tile repeats the image over and over to fill the space. Center positions the image in the middle of the desktop and surrounds the unfilled space with black.

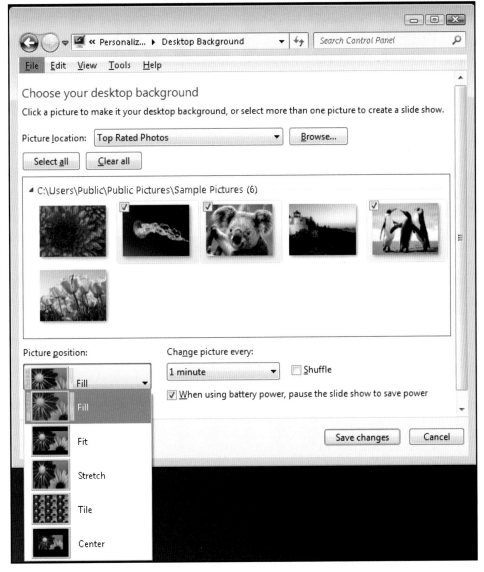

Figure 7.5

9. To rotate the picture being shown from among several you've selected, choose an option, from every 10 seconds to once a day. Click to put a tick in the Shuffle checkbox to cause the images to be shown in random order.

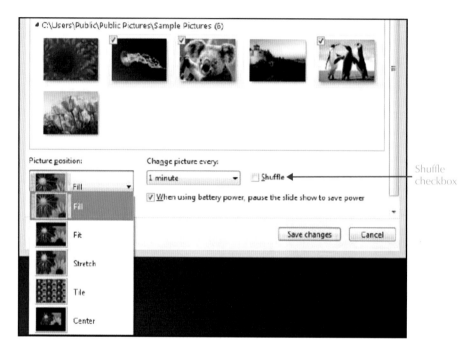

Figure 7.6

This pull-down menu is only available if you've chosen more than one image.

Click Cancel to ignore all the choices you just made and go back to the previous choice. Click OK to use your choices to set the desktop background.

As you can see, even the simple approach involves quite a few steps. The full approach, using or at least considering all the options, takes a lot more steps and a lot more thought. As you get more comfortable with your laptop many of these choices will become second nature. Things that seemed difficult at first will become easy.

Changing the desktop Windows icons

The desktop's role as a catch-all is potentially quite problematic. It includes icons you shouldn't remove – the ones Windows puts there – plus folders, data files and programs. Some of what you see on the desktop are shortcuts, which are links to an actual program, folder or data file; some of the icons are the actual programs, folders and data files themselves.

Safe use of the desktop begins with understanding what the icons are that Windows itself puts there, and deciding what you want to appear. Here are the icons that you can manage using Windows 7:

- **Computer**. This icon represents the physical computer you're using and what's on it and connected to it.

- **Control panel**. The control panel is important, but you don't normally need it on your desktop.

- **User's files**. This icon denotes the files specific to the currently signed-in user, usually (but not always) data files.

- **Network**. This icon is for accessing network connections. You don't normally need this for home use.

- **Recycle Bin**. The recycle bin holds files you've thrown away, which allows you to restore them if needed – with some potentially dangerous exceptions, as I'll describe below.

Here's how to change the icons that are on the desktop:

1. Make the desktop visible.

   If you have windows open obscuring the desktop, click the Show Desktop button on the right edge of the Taskbar, which is usually found at the bottom of the screen.

2. Right-click on an open part of the desktop.

   A context-sensitive menu appears showing options for the desktop.

3. Click the bottom option on the menu, Personalize.

   The Personalization control panel appears.

Recycle bin

Figure 7.7

You can also personalise the desktop by going directly through Windows Control Panels, but it's easier to remember to begin personalising it by right-clicking on it.

4. Click the option, Change desktop icons.

    The Desktop Icon Settings dialogue box appears.

5. Click the checkboxes until the options you want are selected (shown by a tick mark in the box).

    I recommend that you keep core icons on the desktop such as Computer, Documents and Recycle Bin. However, if you plan to use the desktop for accessing the laptop's functions a lot, include User's Files and Control Panel. If you are running a network, include the remaining option, Network, as well.

6. Click Apply.

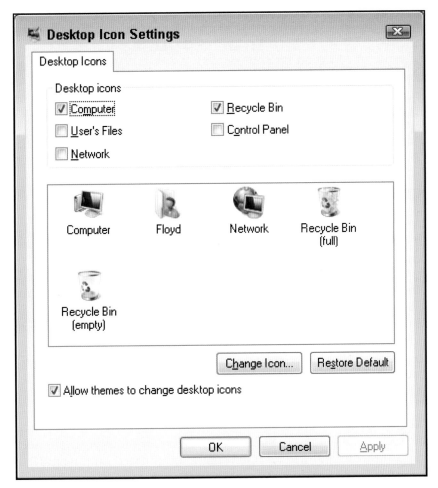

Figure 7.8

The desktop will be updated with the choices you've made.

7. Click OK.

The dialogue box closes.

8. In the Personalization control panel, click the X in the upper right-hand corner to close it.

The control panel closes.

In these steps I describe a setup for a single user. If you want to use a multi-user setup, it can get a bit complicated as to who can do what and when. It's easy for the computer to seem broken because some users can't get to things others can. I recommend you to another resource such as *Windows 7 for Dummies* (ISBN 9780470497432) if you want to use a multi-user setup on your laptop or learn how to use your laptop in more detail.

Using the Recycle Bin

The Windows desktop has more capabilities than I can explain here, but the Recycle Bin is worth a brief mention. It's also a good example of how many Windows capabilities work.

The Recycle Bin is a rubbish bin for your unused computer files. You don't normally get rid of programs through the Recycle Bin; this is done by installing and uninstalling them using a control panel. Usually the Recycle Bin is used to get rid of shortcuts and data files.

You can specify the size of the Recycle Bin. Just right-click on it and choose Properties. You can then change three options for the Recycle Bin:

- **The size of the Recycle Bin**. Set the size of the Recycle Bin in megabytes. Any space in the Recycle Bin is not available for other programs and files. If you want to set the size to 1GB – not a lot of space on a typical 160GB or larger hard disk – enter 1024 as the number of megabytes.

- **Whether to keep files in the Recycle Bin**. Normally files you keep in the Recycle Bin stay there until you deliberately delete the files in the Recycle Bin. The ability to 'rescue' files is often a godsend. However, it can also interfere with your privacy, as others can 'rescue' your files too. You can also set the Recycle Bin to immediately delete files, making them inaccessible to anyone (including you). In this case the Recycle Bin doesn't consume any space on your hard disk.

- **Whether to ask before deleting anything**. The option to ask before deleting anything is called 'Display delete confirmation dialog'. The Recycle Bin normally asks you before deleting anything, which can also be a godsend. You can turn this off, but I don't recommend doing so.

Normally the Recycle Bin with the usual settings – fairly large, perhaps 1GB; set to store files so you can rescue them if needed; and set to ask before finally deleting anything – is your friend. You will probably rescue files from it more than once.

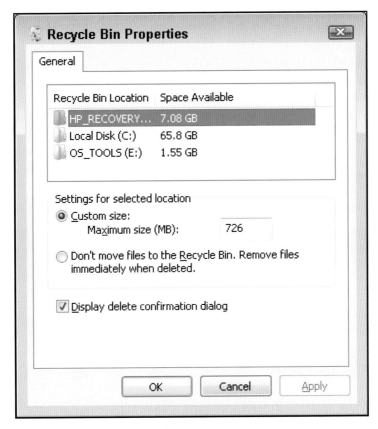

Figure 7.9

Care with the Recycle Bin

You can easily get into the habit of moving things to the Recycle Bin rather lightly, secure in the knowledge they can be restored if needed. However, there are two instances where the Recycle Bin will delete things instantly, even if you've set it up not to. Both instances tend to occur when you would least want them to.

The first instance is when the Recycle Bin is overfull. The Recycle Bin is quite large, so this only tends to occur when you move very large things into it, such as folders full of (possibly precious) photos or a copy of all or most of your data files. Sometimes what you've moved is the one and only copy, or the most recent copy. In these cases, the Recycle Bin will ask (if that's the way you've set it up) whether it should completely delete the files immediately. It's quite easy to say 'Yes' to the request and then, as your one and only copy of important files is instantly deleted, to say 'Nooooo!'

The other instance is when file and folder names get too long for the Recycle Bin to deal with. When you have folders, in folders, in folders and so on, combined with very long file names – common when you save web pages to your hard disk, for instance – the combination of the folder and file names gets too long for Windows to handle. When you move such files to your hard disk, the Recycle Bin will ask you if you want to delete the entire folder immediately, even if only one single file has a name that's too long. Again, it's easy to say 'Yes' when you shouldn't have.

Never throw away the Documents folder on your desktop in the Recycle Bin. You could lose a lot of important files. (I speak from experience.)

I've had this latter problem happen to me recently. I was cleaning up my desktop and accidentally deleted the Documents file. In Windows XP, which I've used for nearly ten years, the crucial folder is called My Documents, and I knew not to ever delete that. In the newer Windows 7, though, it's simply called Documents, which sounded a bit generic and unimportant to me. I deleted all my documents, and was only able to recover most (not all) of them after a frantic online search for information, paying to purchase a special program, and several hours of work.

As with the Recycle Bin, you can see the Properties of many different icons on the Windows desktop by right-clicking on them and choosing Properties from the context-sensitive menu that appears. Sometimes the Properties are just a description of the file, such as its name and size. Other times the Properties include important aspects of the underlying file, folder or program that you can control. Keep inspecting the Properties of various items until you get a feel for what your options are.

Starting any program

The Start menu gives you access to all your programs via shortcuts, links to the actual program stored on your hard disk.

As you'll see, many unimportant programs are shown right up front, easy to access. Yet vital Microsoft tools are stored in the Accessories folder, or even a subfolder of Accessories such as System Tools, where they're harder to find.

Programs that you pay money for, such as Microsoft Office, are typically shown in a folder, so that you have to click to open the folder and look around for a program such as Microsoft Word that you might use every day.

You can reduce this problem by copying shortcuts to important programs to the desktop, the Start menu or the Taskbar, as described below.

If you delete shortcuts from the Start menu, it will no longer give you access to all your programs. You will then have to find the program on your hard disk, which is not easy. So I recommend that you never delete shortcuts from the Start menu.

To start any program on your system, follow these steps:

1. Click the Start button.

   The Start Menu opens.

2. Click All Programs.

   This option is in the lower left of the Start menu.

   A list of all the programs on your laptop – usually a very long list – appears in a narrow column. Programs appear on three levels: The program may appear directly in the list; it may appear in a folder that usually has a name similar to the name of the program; or it may appear in the Accessories folder, which contains small programs sometimes called utilities, or even a subfolder of Accessories.

3. Click the shortcut of the program you want to run.

   The program will start.

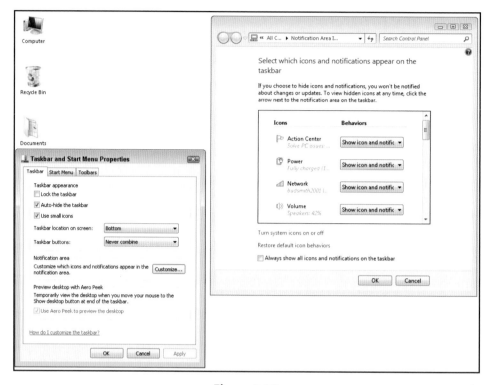

Figure 7.10

 As soon as you start a program, a new shortcut to it appears in the recently accessed programs area of the Start menu. See the next section for instructions on how to pin the shortcut to the Start menu, retaining it for the long term.

Changing the Start menu

The Start menu gives you access to all your programs and data files. You can set it to make access to programs quite quick.

Every user's Start menu is different. That's because of three things that gradually occur as you use your computer:

- The most recent programs you use appear in your Start menu, displacing programs you haven't used for a while.

- Some programs are 'pinned', or fixed, to the upper part of your Start menu before you get your laptop and, as you use it, other programs you install pin themselves there as well. (Nearly every program you install has an option set to pin itself to your start menu; you have to clear the option if you want to prevent it happening.)

- You directly intervene, pinning some items and unpinning others to customise your Start menu.

The upper area of the Start Menu shows pinned programs; the lower part (whatever area remains after pinned programs are accounted for) shows the most recent programs you've used that aren't pinned.

You can use the upper part of the Start menu as a quick access area to your favourite programs. Here's how to change the upper part of the Start menu:

1. Find a program or shortcut icon.

   One of the easiest places to find a program or shortcut icon is in the Start menu's lower part, which has all recently launched programs not already in the upper part of the Start menu.

2. Right-click the program or shortcut icon.

   Options for the program or shortcut appear. If the program is not already pinned to the upper area of the Start menu, pinning it there will be an option. (If the program is already pinned, you'll be given the choice to unpin it instead.)

You can also personalise the desktop by going directly through Windows Control Panels, but it's easier to remember to begin personalising it by right-clicking on it.

3. Choose the option, Pin to Start menu.

   A shortcut for the program is pinned to the Start menu.

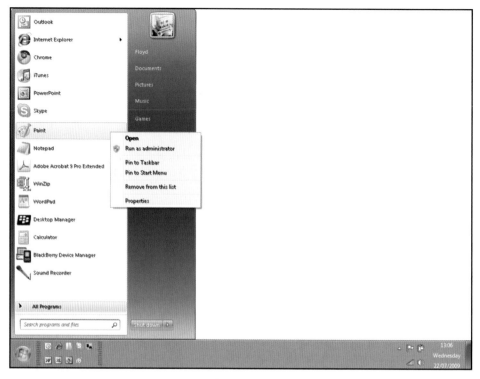

Figure 7.11

You can also directly manipulate the programs pinned to the Start menu. Drag and drop them to change the order. The goal is to end up with a short list of your favourite programs in an order that makes sense to you. Once you've established this, and stop changing it, accessing your favourite programs will gradually become automatic.

Changing the Taskbar

The Taskbar always shows three things: the Start button; currently running programs, each as a button on the Taskbar; and Notifications. This brief section describes what you can do with the main part of the Taskbar, between the Start menu (described above) and the Notifications (described below).

The Taskbar is always useful for moving amongst your currently running programs. With each having its own button on the Taskbar, you can quickly see what's running and jump between them.

There's a subtle distinction here that makes a big difference. You can have all your open windows for a given program, for example, your Microsoft Word documents, combined into a single button. Hover over the button to see a list of the separate open windows.

Alternatively, you can have each open window occupy its own button. I favour this method.

You can also use the Taskbar as a supplement or alternative to the Start menu, making it a launching area for programs you use frequently. There are two ways to do this:

● Open a sub-menu to the Taskbar called the Links area and drag shortcuts into there. Recommended.

● Pin programs directly to the Taskbar, where the program icon appears intermixed with the buttons for currently running programs. Pinning programs to the Taskbar is very similar to pinning them to the Start menu; right-click on a program link and choose Pin to taskbar.

Moving programs to the Links area requires that you first open the Links area, described below. Then drag a program shortcut from elsewhere – the desktop or the Start menu are two options – to the Links area. The shortcut will be copied, creating a new shortcut in the Links area.

You can change some things about the Taskbar by direct manipulation. Try these tricks:

● **Grab** the edge of the Taskbar where it intersects with the Desktop. Drag it up and down. The Taskbar will resize. I keep the Taskbar two icons high so it shows a lot of information.

● **Click** in the middle of the Taskbar and drag it to another edge of the screen. It can 'live' on the left, right, top or bottom edge. (I almost never see it placed anywhere except the bottom though, so you'll be unusual if you put it elsewhere, but it's all down to personal preference.)

● **Drag** and drop buttons for open programs around to put them into a sensible order. (I used to start programs in a certain order to make this happen until I discovered I could move the buttons directly.)

To change further options for the Taskbar, right-click the Taskbar and choose Properties. (This practice of right-clicking and choosing Properties should be starting to sound familiar!) The Taskbar and Start Menu Properties will appear with the Taskbar tab selected.

Here are brief descriptions of some of the many options for customising the Taskbar from within the Taskbar tab:

- **Lock the taskbar**. Prevents you from changing the taskbar size and moving it around. Great if you are nervous about changing things, or if you occasionally let grandchildren and so on use your computer.

- **Auto-hide the taskbar**. Makes the taskbar go away except when you hover over the lower edge of the screen. This buys you valuable screen space, but makes the screen a bit too dynamic for some of us.

- **Use small icons**. You have the option to make the icons smaller. This can make more space on the desktop, but it can make them more difficult to read.

- **Taskbar location on screen:** Can be set to Bottom, Left, Right or Top. Where you have the Taskbar is up to you, but the default and the common favourite is by far the bottom of the screen.

- **Taskbar buttons**. When I have several Word documents open, I like to have a separate button for each document, so I choose Never combine for the taskbar buttons. You can also choose Always combine or Combine when taskbar is full.

To use a Links area for programs in the Taskbar follow these steps:

1. Right-click on the Taskbar and choose Properties. In the Taskbar and Start Menu Properties dialogue box which appears, choose the Toolbars tab.

2. Click Links to turn on the Links toolbar within the Taskbar.

3. Drag the Links area to where you want it.

4. Drag shortcuts into the Links area to populate it.

5. Right-click in the Links area to set labelling options for the Links area.

    You will now have a new link on your Taskbar.

Changing the Notifications area

The Notifications area contains visible icons of vital concern for a laptop user: remaining power and wireless access. Speaker volume on or off can be pretty important too, for instance when a Web page suddenly starts playing a loud video or audio clip in a previously quiet café.

If a system icon is turned off, you will never see it or get the chance to change its behaviour. Follow the steps below to ensure that all system icons are turned on so you can modify them.

Along with a vital few notifications from Windows itself, the Notifications area can also display other Windows notifications and notifications from other programs, which most of us would consider far less important. There might be something in there, though, of particular concern to you.

As such, it's important to customise the Notification area so it shows the crucial few Windows system notifications, plus any others you want. Follow these steps:

1. Right-click in the Taskbar.

   The Taskbar and Start Menu Properties dialogue appears with the Taskbar tab to the fore. In the middle of the tab you'll see the Notification area.

2. Click the button, Customize.

   Alternatively, click the tiny triangle on the edge of the Notifications area. The Control Panel called Notification Area Icons appears.

3. Click the link, Turn system icons on or off. I recommend that you turn them all on.

The system icons: Clock, Volume, Network, Power and Action Center are listed, along with a choice of Behavior for each. I recommend that you choose On for all of them. (Clock may seem unimportant, but you often need to see the system's idea of the time to determine, for instance, if a file was created within the last few minutes.)

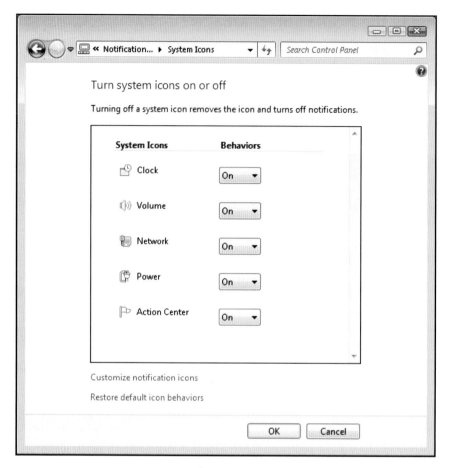

Figure 7.12

4. Click the link, Customize notification options, to return to the list of available icons and behaviours.

   The main area of the control panel will reappear.

5. Choose options, called Behaviours, for each icon. For important icons, choose Show icon and notifications. For less important icons, choose Only show notifications. For unimportant icons, choose Hide icon.

   I recommend that you choose the most visible option, Show icon and notifications, for these key icons: Action Center, which can show important Windows system messages; Power, which shows whether you're plugged in and battery charge level; Network, which shows wireless network strength;

and Volume, which shows the current speaker volume level. For others, I suggest you choose Only Show Notifications.

6. I recommend that you leave the option, Always show all icons and notifications on the taskbar, unchecked.

    There's a lot of trivia that would show up if you always showed all icons and notifications. Also, you can always click the little triangle in the Notifications area to show hidden icons.

> Double-click on almost any item to open it or see further options for it. Double-click on the wireless networks icon to see currently available networks; double-click on the date area to see options for displaying it.

Desktop strategies

Now that you've seen many of the options for customising your overall desktop – the open desktop itself, the Start menu and the Taskbar – you may realise the need for some sort of consistent approach to the whole thing. Otherwise, you could end up starting different programs in different ways and it might become a bit confusing.

Here I'll make the case briefly for primarily using each of the several different options:

- **The desktop**. You can easily put program links on the desktop and start programs from there. You can also add all sorts of tools; see Desktop Gadgets in the next section. To get all the open windows out of the way, click the Show desktop button on the right edge of the Taskbar. To put all your windows back in place, click the same button again.

- **The Start menu**. If you store your favourite programs in the Start menu, your shortlist of programs is one click away, and the long list is available from the same general location. The Start menu is the easiest shortlist of programs to manage.

- **The Taskbar**. Whether you pin programs to the main Taskbar or, my favourite, the Links toolbar on the taskbar, your shortlist of programs is always visible. It doesn't change unless and until you change it. It's not as easy to set up as the other options, but once you do it's a true power user's tool.

The choice is up to you.

What about the Mac?

I've largely ignored the Mac here, partly because Windows is still the market leader, but also partly because using the Mac is both simpler and less flexible, so needs less explanation.

Consistent with its overall approach, the Mac has setup wizards that take you through the steps similar to those I've described here for Windows. The Apple website has helpful videos describing the steps as well. It would be impossible for Microsoft to fully match this integrated support, as the many different PC makers who use Windows each configure it slightly differently.

The Mac's Taskbar equivalent is called the Dock, which is a more consistent approach than I've described here. Backup – one of the crucial functions for using a computer, and a source of so many disasters for users – is prominently featured. The Mac is less configurable, but more consistent and many feel more helpful, than the Windows equivalent.

If you are familiar with Windows, but are considering moving to a Mac, Apple keeps some useful resources on its website for making the transition.

Setting up

Once you decide on an approach, implement it. That is, find the programs you think you'll use regularly and put shortcuts to them on the desktop; on the Start menu; or on the Taskbar.

To create a shortcut, find a program or a shortcut to it, then create a shortcut. Follow these steps:

1. Find the program or shortcut you want.

    Go to the Start menu, click Programs, and from there you will find the program you want to create a shortcut to.

2. Right-click on your chosen program to bring up the context-sensitive menu. Choose Pin to Taskbar or Pin to Start Menu.

    This causes a shortcut to be created. If your goal is to put the shortcut on the desktop, choose Pin to Taskbar. Then drag the shortcut out of the Taskbar onto the desktop.

3. Build up a set of shortcuts to the programs you plan to use regularly.

   This can take some thought, but remember that you can always edit the list when you need to.

 Limit the number of programs you keep in your working set on the desktop, Start menu or Taskbar. Remember that the average person can keep four to seven things in short-term memory, and Top Ten lists are popular. In creating your working set of programs, try to keep it to ten or even fewer; for other programs, you can always start them from the Start menu. I'm a very active computer user and I usually have about nine programs and a link to the Documents folder in the Links area of my Taskbar.

Control Panel

If you're particularly astute, you may have noticed that many of the options I've mentioned so far in this chapter are really different ways of accessing Control Panels. You may have wondered what Control Panels are and if there are more of them.

The answers are: 1) Control Panels are Windows' way of managing system settings, and 2) yes, there are many more of them.

To access all the control panels, choose Start ⇨ Control Panel.

Windows shows you a nicely arranged array of 20 control panels under eight different categories. There are also many more of them. If you choose View by: and either Small icons or Large icons, you'll see a complete list of control panels. Although the total will vary a bit by the specific system you're using and what's loaded on it, you're likely to see about 50 control panels!

This is too many to deal with constructively; if you were to spend 10 minutes with each of them, that would be a full day's work. That's why I've encouraged you to access Control Panels directly through specific areas of Windows as you need them; the top-down approach could be overwhelming.

Here's a brief summary of some of the most important Control Panels:

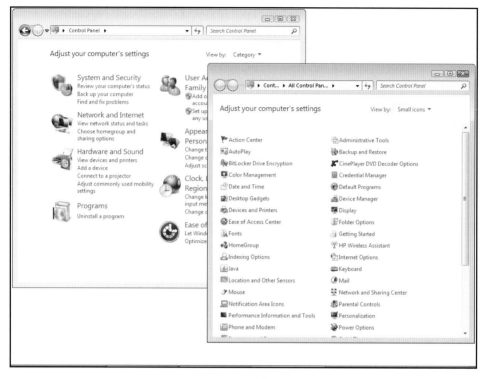

Figure 7.13

- **Action Center, Notification Area Icons, Personalization, Sound, Date and Time, Taskbar and Start Menu.** All of these are very useful, and are mentioned above.

- **Folder options.** The specific way folders work can make quite a difference in how you handle data files in particular. Try changing these, but note the Restore Defaults button if you get in trouble; it takes you back to where you started.

- **Desktop Gadgets.** You can put all kinds of things on your Windows desktop, and Desktop Gadgets is where you can get access to them.

- **System.** Among other options, this control panel leads to the Device Manager, where you can directly control settings for devices that are part of, or attached to, your system. This gives you a lot of power, but can be quite complicated as well.

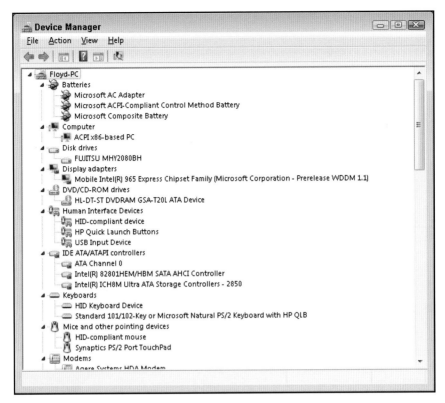

Figure 7.14

Some people enjoy tinkering with features such as the Control Panels. If you are one of them, the Control Panels can provide many hours of fun, while making you a much better Windows user as well. However, in all likelihood you are likely to be one of the vast majority of folk who simply want their laptop to work.

I do recommend you tour the Control Panels just to get a feel for what's there, so you have a bit of familiarity when problems or new activities send you back to them in the future. An interesting, if baffling, way to spend an hour or so!

Summary

- Using either the Mac or Windows is based around the idea of a 'desktop' on which you put various things you use – both information (files and folders) and tools (programs). You grab and manipulate things with a mouse or track pad.

- Windows, more than the Mac, is highly 'configurable' – you can change the way it works to suit your desires.

- On either system you can change the desktop background, even creating a slide show from among your photos that will 'play' across the desktop.

- The Recycle Bin in Windows is quite important; take care when deleting files from here.

- You can use any or all of the following as a launch pad for computer programs: the desktop, the Start menu or the Taskbar.

Brain Training

There may be more than one correct answer to these questions.

1. What's the most recent version of Windows?

a) Windows 95

b) Windows XP

c) Windows 7

d) Windows Vista

2. Where can you launch programs from in Windows?

a) The desktop

b) The Start button

c) The All Programs menu within the Start button

d) The Taskbar

3. What can you not do with photos in Windows 7?

a) Put a photo on the desktop

b) Put a slide show of photos on the desktop

c) Have your photos stretch to fill the desktop

d) Have the desktop 'morph' your photo with others

4. What are key icons to keep visible in the Taskbar?

a) Recycle Bin size

b) Wireless network status

c) Folder settings

d) Power status

5. What do you call onscreen dialogue for changing Windows system settings?

a) Synthesizers ('synths' for short)

b) Heads-up displays

c) Control Panels

d) Chords

Answers

Q1 – c   **Q2** – all of them   **Q3** – d   **Q4** – b and d

Q5 – c

PART III
Getting up and running

I hate drinking the stuff —but it's the only place around here where I can get online...

©2009 Stephen Long

Getting power to the people

8

Equipment needed: a laptop

Skills needed: Basic knowledge of the keyboard, mouse and operating system to try options and change settings (see Chapter 7).

Surveys show that battery life is the number one concern of laptop buyers. The main appeal of a laptop is freedom and independence. Therefore, it can be somewhat frustrating to worry about your battery power, or to have your battery die when you are out and about.

Keeping your laptop powered is easy when you're using it at home with the laptop plugged into the mains. (See Chapter 6 for more information on creating a comfortable and safe home setup.)

The tricky part is when you go on the move, whether it's just out to the balcony, or visiting friends and family. Then you'll face two challenges: keeping your machine going on battery power in between periods when you have mains access, and keeping a wireless connection for as much of the time as possible.

You can typically expect your laptop to run for more than two hours after you unplug. The trick is: how much more? You can find out by running your laptop without power while using it normally at home. Then you can improve your laptop's battery life using the tips and tricks in this chapter.

A related, 'green' reason for minimising power and battery usage is that it saves electricity. Recharging a battery uses roughly twice as much energy as simply running from mains power. Keep in mind, though, that a laptop, somewhat amazingly, only uses about as much power as a light bulb, and much less than a desktop.

'Green IT', as it's called, is a big topic overall, though. Power savings that are small on an individual basis become large when multiplied over thousands of users in a corporation or millions of purchasers of popular models of laptops. The manufacturing, use and disposal of computers has a very large environmental impact. Computer and software producers are taking steps to reduce their carbon footprint to minimise environmental damage.

With both the planet and the usefulness of your laptop in mind, I'll tell you how to use your computer with less power consumption and how to find places to plug into mains power whenever possible. In the next chapter I'll tell you how to get a wireless connection in a surprising variety of places.

If you're looking for the nitty-gritty of how to change power management options, that's at the end of the chapter. First I explain what's going on so you understand what you're accomplishing with the options.

How long does your laptop run without power?

Magazines and other reviewers typically test battery life by playing a DVD on the laptop with screen brightness on full and simultaneously running a program that keeps the computer's 'brains' and hard disk working. This is a fair test, but a harsh one. That means it's a useful comparison between laptops, but probably uses up the battery quicker than you would doing normal work.

Try running your laptop without mains power while at home and see how long it lasts. For this test, keep everything turned on – the screen on normal brightness and so on, just as if you were plugged in. See how long your system lasts before you run out of power.

How your laptop uses power

To get the most out of your laptop's battery life, it's good to know how it uses power.

Luckily, we don't have to guess. Engineers at Microsoft, working on the Windows 7 operating system, did extensive research on how current laptops use power. They used the results to improve power management in Windows 7. (The results apply, for the most part, to all laptops, not just those running Windows 7.)

They produced a chart that shows typical power use for laptops (Figure 8.1).

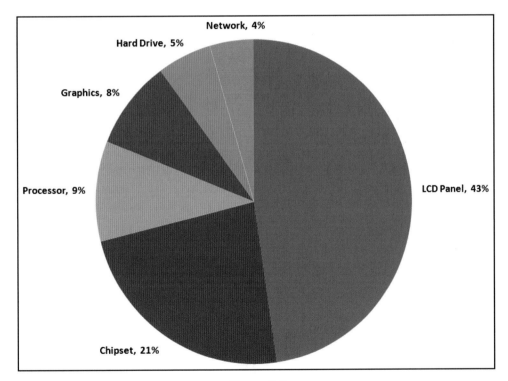

Figure 8.1

● **LCD Panel and graphics**. Those big, bright, beautiful screens that laptops are famous for are the biggest single user of power in a laptop, at about 43%.

(Your mileage will vary.) Graphics chips, which keep the screen image updated, use another 8%, for a total of 51% – half your laptop's battery usage.

The implication? Turning your screen brightness down is the single biggest way to extend battery life; turning the screen off when you're not using your laptop, even for a few minutes, is the biggest power-saver of all.

● **Processor and chipset**. The processor, or CPU, is the brains of your computer, and the chipset is the chips that keep it supplied with information and carry out its commands. At 21% of power usage for the chipset and 9% for the processor, they use a total of 30%, nearly a third of your laptop's power usage. Unfortunately, these chips use power even when they're not doing anything, though less than when they're active.

The implication? Laptop processors and chipsets are getting ever smaller and less power-hungry; the key innovation is that the processor turns itself off when it is left idle for even a brief period. (This causes a very slight pause when the processor has to restart.) Putting your laptop into sleep mode is a good way to signal to these internal chips that they can go into low-power mode for a while.

● **Hard drive, network and other**. At a total of 9%, plus 10% unaccounted for, keeping your laptop's hard drive and wireless networking running takes up a relatively small amount of your power budget. Given that the hard disk is the only moving part in the entire system, spinning at thousands of revolutions per second, it's amazing that it uses as little power as it does.

The implication? People managing their laptop's power usage have paid huge attention to keeping the hard disk quiet, but at only 5% of power usage, it isn't worth very much attention. Same with networking; if you can get a wireless connection, there's only a little benefit to your system's battery life in shutting it off.

There are two different elements to reducing your power usage:

● Active steps you take yourself, including simple steps such as turning the computer off when you're not using it.

● Setup steps, setting Windows options to have components automatically turn off when you're not using them.

The best active steps for minimising your computer's power use are simple:

- Turn down the monitor brightness to the lowest comfortable level while working.

- Turn the monitor brightness all the way down when you're not using the computer, even briefly. (Your Windows options should be set to turn it off completely quite soon after that.)

- Use sleep mode to put the entire computer into a quiet state when you're not using the laptop for more than a few minutes. (Likewise, your Windows options should be set to make this happen automatically.)

What happens when you run out of power?

I've actually had a laptop totally run out of power. Nothing really bad happens; it's exactly like doing a complete shut down, which you should do at least once a day. The only problem is that, if you have files open, you'll lose any work you haven't saved – just as if you were using a desktop computer with no battery back-up and accidentally turned off the mains power switch at the wall.

However, laptops are supposed to be too smart for this. When your battery runs very low, and after warning you at least once, the laptop uses a last little bit of power to save the current status to the hard disk, then hibernates – goes into a very low-power mode. You can't use the computer anymore until you plug it in, but you shouldn't lose your work as long as you plug the computer back in within a day or so. (If you leave it too long, even the minimal power used in hibernate mode will drain the remaining battery, the computer will completely halt and you'll lose your work.)

So don't worry about anything horrible happening when the power level drops; you may experience the inconvenience of having to stop using your computer, but you won't damage it, and it's unlikely you'll even lose the work you were doing.

Figure 8.2

Sleep, hibernate and shut down

One of the biggest annoyances I find with most laptops is the fact they don't allow you to turn off the monitor with a switch. When using a desktop system, I turn off the monitor all the time while taking a phone call, stepping away from my desk etc., no doubt saving a fair amount of energy.

I suppose I should put the laptop into Sleep mode, but, perhaps like you, I worry about something happening to my work. Turning off the monitor is a good intermediate step, but I can't easily do it on my laptop.

You can turn off your laptop in three different ways, all of which are located in the Start menu, ironically.

● **Sleep**. Sleep turns off your monitor and tells the hard disk it can stop spinning and the internal components that they can stop running. Like you when you go to sleep, your laptop's power usage drops by perhaps 80% or more. (One measurement on a laptop had it using 15W when fully turned on, but not being used, and only 1W in sleep mode.) However, in the unlikely event that your laptop's power completely runs out while it's in sleep mode, you'll lose any work you had going. Put your laptop in Sleep mode any time you stop using it for even a few minutes; it should revive in about 2 seconds.

- **Hibernate**. Hibernate causes your laptop to burn a bit of power to save its current state of operations, then shuts it down more completely, reducing power usage by nearly (but not quite) 100%. This mode is named 'hibernate' to remind one of a bear hibernating through the winter, using very little energy; almost 0W. The computer is supposed to be able to recover your desktop session even if it runs completely out of power, but I'd try this on a given laptop before I believed it. Hibernate your laptop if you're going to stop using it from anywhere from five minutes up to an hour or more.

- **Shut down**. Before shutting down your laptop you have to close all your open files, and your computer uses a fair amount of power shutting down and starting up again. Also importantly, you lose the context of what you were doing. However, once shut down, you run zero risk of losing unsaved data. Shut down your computer when you won't be using it for an hour or more.

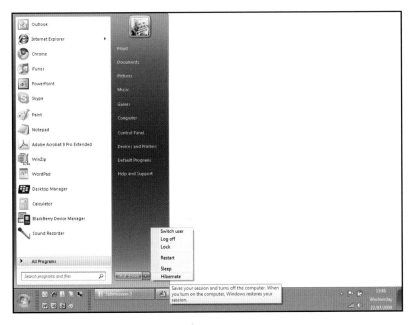

Figure 8.3

Laptops vary in how easy and reliable they are in coming out of Sleep and Hibernate modes. Test Sleep and Hibernate modes on your laptop with several windows open, but nothing too important unsaved. Also try closing the computer's lid – does it Sleep or Hibernate? Does it revive itself properly when you open it? This testing will help you identify any problems in the process of shutting down and restarting your computer and avoid frustration when you really do need to save power.

Should I always just 'sleep' my computer?

It's much faster and more convenient to have your computer 'sleep' or even hibernate between sessions vs. shutting it down and starting it up completely; not only do you save time, but you keep whatever you were doing accessible in the next section. However, 'sleep' still uses a small amount of power, so it's better for both cost reasons and for the environment to hibernate or shut down completely. Of the two, it's better to shut down completely because your computer only completely clears its memory when you're shut down, and it performs certain checks during a full startup that it doesn't perform any other time. Your system will be more stable if you shut down completely at least once a day. (Web browser windows in particular seem to benefit from being closed and having a full shutdown and startup cycle take place.)

If you accidentally put your laptop into Hibernate (by choosing the wrong shut down option, or by closing the lid far enough that it acts as if you closed it all the way) it will take some time to finish hibernating, about 20 seconds on my system. If you panic and push the power button during this time, you'll cut off power suddenly, which will probably mean changes in your open files will be lost. This will also completely confuse your computer, possibly leading to real system problems. So, if you suspect your computer is going into Hibernate, wait a full minute, or for the power indicator to turn off, before pressing any buttons.

Getting an extra battery

An ancient solution to solving problems is to throw money at them. Getting an extra battery for your laptop is the 'throwing money' approach to reducing laptop power problems. I've used this approach with great success in the past while travelling internationally as a consultant, with frequent trips between the UK and New Zealand – about as long a flight as one can take. I was a real 'road warrior', dependent on my laptop for productivity and earnings. In this scenario, an extra battery – paid for by my employer – made sense.

I don't recommend getting an extra battery if you are using the laptop for general use, though. Here are the reasons:

- **Cost**. Extra laptop batteries are specific to the laptop you buy, so there's not an open, competitive market for them. Manufacturers, and the few specialist makers out there, are selling to a small market of people who have few other options, so they charge top dollar. Don't be surprised to be asked for £100 or more for a long-life, 9-cell extra battery.

- **Inconvenience between trips**. You have to keep the standard battery and any extra batteries fully charged all the time so you're ready to go at short notice. I've had trips more or less ruined because I wasn't ready with fully charged batteries when it was time to go.

- **Weight and hassle during trips**. Engineers slave for hours to cut ounces from the weight of your laptop, and then you go and spoil it by toting an extra battery weighing a couple of pounds. In addition to adding to the weight you carry, the extra battery adds bulk, and it's a clumsy piece to fit into a bag. If you lose it, it's expensive to replace.

- **Are you tough enough?** Actually using up all that extra battery life means continuing to use your laptop when few other people are. I've spent many long and lonely hours on international flights as the only person with the overhead light on whilst others tried to sleep around me, grumbling about my rudeness. I was certainly the only person with a laptop when I travelled the Trans-Siberian Railway across half of Russia – which means about a quarter of the planet – trying to get work done when others were asleep or relaxing. In most of these situations, you won't have wireless access anyway, reducing your effectiveness and any 'fun factor' of using your laptop. Perhaps it's best to join others in sleeping, admiring the tundra or whatever else they're doing.

I'm not travelling to New Zealand much these days and I don't have an extra battery for my current laptop. I use my laptop a bit less and enjoy everything else life has to offer a bit more.

That doesn't mean, though, that an extra battery (Figure 8.4) isn't right for some people. If you know of situations where you will be on the road for hours, in a position to use a laptop, and will either have wireless access, or not need it, consider the extra battery as an option.

Some laptops, including most recent Mac laptops, have sealed-in batteries that you can't access. Check what battery your computer uses before purchasing a new battery.

You'll probably need to search online for a battery. Shop carefully; they're expensive items, and must be well made to deliver the battery life you need.

Buy batteries of any sort only from a reputable manufacturer. Batteries contain both flammable and corrosive materials. If a battery is poorly made, this could result in acid leakage or fire.

Power management and Windows 7

Computer hardware and software advance in tandem, each spurring innovation in each other. Sometimes, however, the dance partners miss a step.

Intel and its main competitor in making computer processors, AMD, have been steadily advancing the state of the art in power management for microprocessors and the chipsets that serve them. Microsoft's Vista operating system, however, did not effectively take advantage of the advances. It used more power than the previous version, Windows XP, partly because it required so much more computer memory even for basic operations.

Vista's power management controls were inflexible and not well suited to the needs of hardware manufacturers. The Aero interface, which made the Vista desktop more attractive-looking than under Windows XP, seemed to be a power hog. 'It's a little scary' was how one engineer described Vista's power usage. Hewlett Packard, one of the very largest computer manufacturers, replaced Vista's power management capabilities with software it wrote itself.

Hardware device makers didn't help. Device drivers – software that serves as a point of connection between the device and the operating system – running under Vista tended to prevent it from going into sleep mode, subverting a major source of power savings.

Microsoft has devoted a great deal of attention to the issue, and Windows 7 contains significant improvements. Under Windows 7, laptop displays dim quickly, and laptops go into sleep mode by default.

With Windows 7, Bluetooth stays off unless it's needed. Microsoft has worked with its hardware partners to solve the problem of drivers preventing the computer from going into sleep mode.

The battery meter is a fixture in the Notifications area, and clicking it opens the relevant Control Panel without extra steps. This puts power usage front and centre and makes adjustments much easier.

While there's no percentage figure given for the improvement in Windows 7, it should be significant.

To read a discussion of improving battery life under a Windows 7 laptop from a real expert's point of view, see this article on Windows 7 Energy Efficiency on the Web: http://blogs.msdn.com/e7/archive/2009/01/06/windows-7-energy-efficiency.aspx

Power management and the Mac

Apple Stores and the Apple website prominently feature information on the green credentials and battery life of Apple products. Independent reviews support Apple's claims to longer battery life at a given laptop size than competitors running

Windows. If you're considering a Mac, or have gone ahead and purchased one, find out more about how to get the most out of a Mac laptop's battery from Apple.

The thoughtfulness that goes into the design of Macs shows up in an answer to one of the most prominent worries for laptop users: the concern that you, as the user, or some clumsy oaf other than yourself will trip over the laptop's power cord, risking damage to, or even complete breakage of, the laptop itself.

The Mac power cord has a magnetic connection to the computer that easily breaks loose if the cord is pulled or tripped on. The cord goes flying; the Mac doesn't.

The sooner you start taking power-saving steps in your work session the longer your battery will last.

Using power management

Windows 7 power management is easy to access and fairly capable. Understanding all the options, though, takes a bit of study and thought.

Here's a quick guide to the major options. You could easily spend many hours on the subject of power management. So use these quick tips to get most of the potential benefit, then dig deeper online, in books and in magazine articles, if you really want to wring every last bit of life out of your laptop battery.

The current battery charge remaining always shows as a graphic in the Notifications area. (To turn on this icon if it's been turned off, see the previous chapter.) You can get an approximate idea of remaining battery life just by eyeing up the icon. If it looks a bit less than half full, you usually have about an hour of battery life left on most notebooks.

To get the system's estimate of just how long you've got, hover the mouse over the battery icon. An estimated amount of time, down to the minute, and a percentage of battery life remaining appear.

That's the diagnostic part; what if you want to take action? Here is a quick recap on the easy steps you can take to start saving battery life:

- **Dim the screen**. Most laptops give you keyboard controls for this. To save power, try to use the laptop with brightness turned all the way down, but don't give yourself eyestrain.

- **Turn off wireless access if you're not using it**. This should be a keyboard control as well. If not, use the wireless notification icon, as described in the next chapter.

- **Turn off the laptop**. Use the Start menu's Sleep option for even short breaks from the computer, Hibernate for longer ones, and turn the computer off completely whenever you can.

- **Change the power-saving settings**. How to do this is described below.

 Microsoft has taken a lot of criticism for the contradiction inherent in having the Sleep, Hibernate and Shut Down options hanging off, of all things, the Start button. In an effort to simplify things a bit, it's highlighted the Shut down option as the default, making you work a bit to get to Sleep and Hibernate. This makes it easy to choose Shut down even when that isn't what you really need. Just as bad, the Restart option – which shuts your computer down, then immediately starts it up again – is right next to Sleep. Which can be slightly annoying if that's not what you wanted to do! Take care when selecting the option you want.

Setting power management options

Let's roll up our sleeves and plunge in; follow these steps to change power management options:

1. Click the battery icon.

   The battery panel appears.

2. Click the link, More power options.

   The Power Options control panel appears.

> 1 hr 10 min (53%) remaining
>
> 14:45
> Monday
> 20/07/2009

Figure 8.4

3. Choose a power management plan. Click Show additional plans to make sure you're shown all available plans.

   Choose the plan most appropriate to your needs. The plans which came with my laptop are Power saver, the stingiest; HP Optimised, which takes a balanced approach; and High performance, which leaves more options on for longer.

4. To change your plan's setting, click any of the following links: Change plan settings (next to the name of the plan), Choose when to turn off the display, or Change when the computer sleeps (both over to the left). All three links do the same thing!

   All three links bring up a new dialogue, Change settings for the plan…with the name of the current plan filled in.

5. Change the power management behaviour of your laptop, concentrating on the settings under 'On battery'.

   See the recommendations in the next section for each setting.

6. Click Save changes to save the changes to the plan.

   The changes will be saved and you'll be returned to the Power Options dialogue.

7. Continue making changes if needed. When you're done, click the X in the upper right corner of the dialogue to close it.

You can view the current screen brightness setting and change it in the Power Options dialogue.

What the main power management options do

There are four main options for Windows power management plans and more than a dozen subsidiary ones.

The four main options are:

● **Brightness** (adjust 1% at a time). This is the option shown last, but is the most important during ongoing use. Most people, frankly, tend to run at full screen brightness whether they need to or not. It's actually easier on your eyes, as well as on your battery life, to run at lower brightness if you can still make out the screen clearly. However, the optimal brightness depends on detailed specifics of the lighting situation where you're using the laptop and your own visual strengths and preferences.

I recommend setting the plan brightness to minimum for all settings so you're always starting from a known starting point. Then, turn the brightness up just as much as needed to achieve a comfortable level.

- **Dim the display** (1 minute up to Never). You should dim the display quite quickly, but it can be annoying to have the display dim on you while you're reading a web page or pausing to think. I find that three minutes is a reasonable interval. (I usually read a page faster than that, and if I'm thinking for that long, I can do it with the screen dimmed.)

- **Turn off the display** (1 minute up to Never). Having the display completely blank on you is, frankly, a bit alarming, and can lead you to think the computer is off when it isn't or to wonder if it's broken. I set the time for this to five minutes to allow me a good amount of time before it happens, while not leaving the screen on forever.

- **Put the computer to sleep** (1 minute up to Never). The effect of this on you when you're using the laptop is not much different than having the screen go blank. Consider setting the time for this quite tightly, to perhaps five or 10 minutes more than the time for turning off the display.

To adjust the brightness by 1% at a time, click the pointer, then use the left or right arrow keys. There are 100 increments of brightness you can set the screen to. The brightness of the display will not change for good until you click the Save changes button.

What advanced power settings do

Windows provides advanced power settings as well as the main ones. To access the advanced settings, click the link, Change advanced power settings, within the Change settings for the plan dialogue.

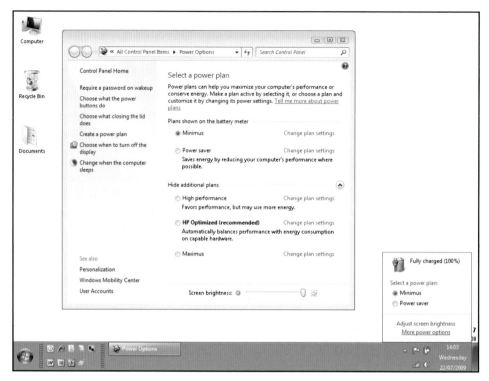

Figure 8.5

These options affect parts of your system that use less than 10% of its power use, so they are probably not worth fooling with unless you are really determined to manage power use down to the level of a couple of percentage points. However, many people would like to do exactly that; if you are one of them, you've come to the right place!

Here are the options provided so you can review and decide which ones to adjust:

- **Hard disk**. Adjust how quickly to turn off the hard disk. It's hard to know all the actions that cause the hard disk to spin up or not. Therefore, it can be equally hard to know just how much this option will affect performance.

- **Wireless adapter settings**. You can adjust your wireless adapter to any of four levels – maximum performance, low power saving, medium power saving and maximum power saving – when on battery or plugged in.

- **Sleep options**. You can set the sleep timer here as well as in the main options and also change the timing for forced hibernation. The default is 1080 minutes (18 hours).

- **USB settings**. This allows USB power to be suspended when not needed. This option should probably only be disabled if it seems to be causing a device connected via USB to stop working.

- **Power buttons and lid**. Here you can set what happens when you close your computer's lid, press the Power button or the Sleep button. Changing these options may just confuse you or anyone who borrows your computer.

- **PCI Express**. Power management settings for PCI cards, such as the cards used for mobile broadband. You can set this to off, moderate power setting or maximum power setting.

- **Processor power management**. You can set the minimum processor state, maximum processor state and system cooling policy. If you set the maximum processor state, to 50%, for instance, you're likely to slow down your system but save energy. Most people will be happy to leave this level of fine-tuning to built-in software and the options set by manufacturers.

- **Display brightness**. As mentioned, changing the display settings can save many useful minutes of battery life.

- **Multimedia settings**. You can turn off the ability of the computer to sleep when sharing media and override power savings efforts when playing a film, so your DVD never dims at a critical moment.

- **Battery**. These options give you very specific control of when low battery warnings appear and when the computer finally hibernates. If you set this too low, the system may not have enough power to carry out the hibernation action, which could make it fail.

The trouble with changing option settings like those given here is that they can cause your system to have unusual problems, or lead you to suspect that these settings have caused a problem when they haven't. It may be better to leave them unchanged unless you're fairly expert in solving power management-related problems as well as other problems. I know my laptop pretty well, and I like having plenty of battery life, but I wouldn't change these options just to get a bit more running time when unplugged.

Creating a power management scheme

You can use the existing power management schemes for most of your needs, adjusting them to fit. You may want to create your own, however.

I like the existing options for my system – Power saver, HP Optimised and High performance. However, I also wanted to have a very low-usage option, for when I want the absolute maximum battery time, and a very high-usage option for when I'm not worried about running out of power and don't want any interruptions to my work. (The high-usage option is also good for testing when I'm having a problem with my laptop and want to be sure it isn't being caused by problems with power management.)

You may want to create your own power management scheme(s) as well. Follow these steps to do so:

1. Click the power icon in the Notifications area.

    The battery panel appears.

2. Click the link, More power options.

    The Power Options control panel appears.

3. Click the link, Create a power plan.

    The Create a power plan dialogue appears.

4. Click the plan you want to use as a starting point.

    The settings in the plan you select will be used as the initial options for your plan. For instance, to create a low-power-usage plan, I started with the existing Power saver option.

5. Enter the plan name, then click Next.

    Trying to decide upon a power management plan name is not what you want to be doing when you're worried about battery life or solving a system problem. Enter a simple, obvious name. (I use Minimus for the lowest-power option and Maximus for the highest.)

    When you click Next, the Change settings for the plan dialogue appears. It's exactly the same as the dialogue when you're changing an existing plan. However, it doesn't include the link to advanced settings.

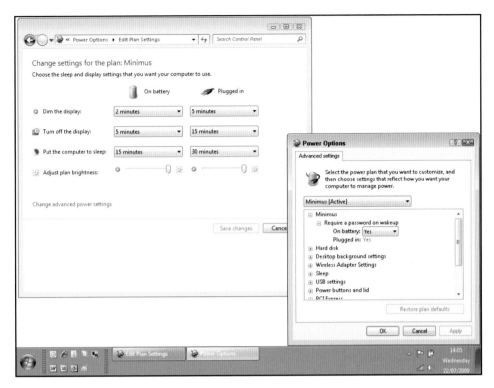

Figure 8.6

6. Change the settings – default screen brightness, how many minutes until dimming the display, how many minutes until turning off the display and how many minutes before putting the computer to sleep. Click Create.

   The plan is created.

7. To further adjust the settings on your new plan, click the link, Change plan settings, next to its name. The plan settings will appear along with the additional options, Change advanced power settings and Delete this plan. Make any additional changes you need, in the main settings or the advanced ones, or delete the plan. Click Save changes or Cancel when you're done.

   The Power Options dialogue appears again.

8. Click the X in the upper right to close the dialogue.

Figure 8.7

Getting plugged in

Power management is important and greatly increases the usefulness of your laptop. However, it's only when you're plugged in that you can, literally, recharge your batteries and not worry about when you're going to run out of power.

Here are a few tips I've tried myself for getting, and staying, plugged in.

● **Carry your power cord with you**. Getting access to mains power does you no good if you don't have your power cord with you, so when in doubt, carry it. Yes, it's a bit heavy and in some cases clumsy, and the prongs on the plug that go into the wall can scratch your laptop's case. Just put the cord in a bag to prevent this. It's all just part of being a laptop owner.

- **Get used to looking for power points**. Once you become a laptop owner yourself, you notice people in public places acting strangely; they're walking around the room looking at the baseboards for a power point they can use for a laptop or mobile phone. Get used to doing this yourself. If all the plugs are taken, ask if you can share. (People about to get on a plane, though, typically won't want to; they may be leaving before you, though, and will usually tell you how long they'll be.)

- **Watch where your cord goes**. It's very easy for people to trip over awkwardly placed cords. It's even easy for you to trip over your own cord. Watch where your cord goes and don't be afraid to give people a friendly warning if they pass near or over your cord. The laptop you save may be your own! (And you may prevent someone from injuring themselves while you're at it.)

- **Check with airlines before flying**. Some airline seats, especially in business class and first class, have plugs for laptops; others don't. Some are traditional British mains plugs, others are to other national standards, and some are cigarette lighter-style. Also, don't be the last one to board, as there are usually fewer sockets than seats.

- **Check with train companies before taking the train**. Many trains have mains power plugs for some seats and some even have free wi-fi. Ask before you travel.

- **Check about plugs and wireless with ferry companies**. A ferry may or may not have plugs and/or wireless access; check before sailing.

- **Gear up**. Get a multi-national adapter plug, which costs just a few pounds, and a cigarette lighter adapter plug for your car, which may be around £20 to £25. Get these before you need them! It can actually be fun to let a family member or friend drive while you work; remember, though, that you won't have wireless access in a car, unless of course you opted for mobile broadband (more about this in chapter 9).

- **When in doubt, plug in**. You may be tempted to let your laptop battery run down before you bother to plug in, but by then, someone else may make use of any available socket. When in doubt, get plugged in.

- **Always keep your computer with you**. You may be tempted to walk away from your laptop to buy a cup of coffee or to totter off to the toilets, but you must keep your laptop with you. Thieves will often be watching the laptop – and you – very closely indeed. Some work in pairs: one to distract you, the other to steal your laptop. Be vigilant!

Having power is important, but of course so is wireless access; see the next chapter for tips and tricks on staying connected whilst you're out and about.

Some of these activities may seem strange at first, and it may seem impolite to ask strangers, for instance, about sharing a plug. In today's world, though, many cafés, train companies and so on understand that power and/or wireless access is helping bring in customers, and they're used to answering questions about it. Your fellow laptop users and mobile phone users are used to sharing power access and are likely to be sympathetic.

Summary

- Power management is a top concern among laptop users. The screen, microprocessor and supporting chips inside a computer use up most of your laptop's power, so manage them closely.

- Putting your computer to sleep, having it hibernate, and shutting it down are progressively stronger steps for saving power.

- Extra batteries add life to your laptop but come with a lot of expense and can be troublesome.

- Windows 7 power management options are quite comprehensive and a big improvement on Windows Vista.

Brain Training

There may be more than one correct answer to these questions.

1. What's the number one concern of laptop buyers?

a) Screen brightness

b) Battery life

c) Back strain from carrying the laptop

d) The weight of a laptop

2. What's the number one consumer of power in a typical laptop?

a) The screen and graphics

b) The processor and RAM

c) The hard disk

d) The wireless Internet circuitry

3. Which shutdown mode takes longest to recover from?

a) Sleep

b) Hibernate

c) Shut down

d) Null mode

4. Is getting an extra-capacity battery worth the cost and hassle?

a) Almost always

b) Sometimes

c) Rarely

d) Yes, if your employer is paying for it

5. What are some good ideas for plugging in away from home?

a) Keep your eyes peeled for power points

b) Check with travel companies about power point availability before embarking on your trip

c) Don't plug in until your battery's nearly dead

d) Plug in the laptop when you see a convenient powerpoint to keep the battery at full strength

Answers

Q1 – b   **Q2** – a   **Q3** – c   **Q4** – c and d

Q5 – a, b, and d

Staying connected

9

Equipment needed: A laptop with wireless Internet access.

Skills needed: Basic knowledge of the keyboard, mouse and operating system to try further options and settings (see Chapters 7 and 8).

Having a connection to the Internet was at one time the exclusive privilege of research scientists and the U.S. military. Today it seems everyone and everything is connected, and increasingly those connections are wireless. With your new laptop, there is no need to be tethered to the phone socket via a wire to surf the Internet or send email. In many cases, you can simply use your laptop's wireless capability to access the Internet. In this chapter I discuss how to connect wirelessly in various situations and where to look for a connection when you need one and don't have it.

The roots of the Internet date to the 1960s with the creation of the ARPANET by the U.S. Department of Defense.

Wireless connections at home and away

Ironically, the easiest and best place to use a laptop and wireless access – designed, as both are, for use on the go – is at home. That's largely because you can get low-priced, reliable broadband service for your home that, ideally, works anywhere in the house and even out in the garden if you're lucky. (It's a bit hard to use a laptop in direct sunlight, but under a shady tree might work well.)

You should be able to place your home broadband router anyplace in the house where there's a phone socket. Move the router around if you don't have sufficient coverage. If you like, you can even get an additional router, repeaters and so on to make sure your entire home is covered by your wireless network, but that is not usually necessary.

The great thing about home broadband is that it's usually fairly fast and virtually unlimited in the quantity of data you can transfer. The speeds can be slower than the top speed advertised – you may get 2Mbps (megabits per second) instead of 8Mbps, for instance. Frankly, this is still fast enough for normal use of Web pages, email and so on. Watching a YouTube video or BBC iPlayer online usually works just fine, with only the occasional delay.

With home broadband, even if it isn't always as fast as it should be, the quantity of information you can transfer is virtually unlimited. Some providers have proposed capping usage to stop, or at least slow down, people who host web sites or share audio or video files. Don't worry if you hear of such limits; they shouldn't affect normal usage and would probably improve performance for most users.

You also have the option to use mobile broadband for your Internet access, either regularly or only when you're on the move. If so, you'll avoid some of the hassles described in this chapter, except when you're out of mobile range.

As you propose to set off from the home – or, if you're a mobile broadband user, when your mobile network is unavailable – there are three ways to stay connected:

- Using free broadband services in various places.
- Using paid broadband services in various places.
- Using alternatives for getting online that don't run through your laptop.

A brief description of each technique follows. First, though, I'll show you how to find a wireless network from those available to you.

Use the information in this chapter to look at wireless networks and settings while you're at home with access to your home broadband network. That way you'll be ready to look for and, hopefully, find a usable network when you venture out and about.

Finding and choosing a wireless network

The mechanics of finding and choosing a wireless network are similar to the mechanics of power management described in the previous chapter:

● Find the icon for wireless networks in the Notifications area of your Taskbar.

● Click the icon to see currently available networks in a panel.

● Click a link in the panel to connect to the relevant Control Panel.

I'll take you through each of these steps in detail.

The Network icon in Notifications

The Network icon in Notifications shows your current network status. This can include:

No connections available (which really means either 'No wireless networks available' or 'your wireless circuitry is turned off or broken').

Networks available; you're not yet connected to any of them.

Your laptop is trying to connect to a network but needs a security key, password, payment or some other step to be taken.

At least one network is available, and you're connected to it.

I'll describe each of these situations below.

Not connected – no connections are available

 A red X through the Network icon means there are no connections available.

This occurs in two very different situations. The first is if your wireless connection is turned on and working, but there are no wireless networks within range of your laptop's wireless radio circuitry. This is how most people would understand 'no connections available'.

Confusingly, the same icon appears if your wireless connection is not turned on or is not working. (This is a common problem with computer error messages; they sometimes don't mean what they seem to.) In this case, the error message means almost the opposite of what it says. There may be plenty of wireless connections available. You won't know this, however, until you get your wireless networking going, because your machine won't be able to access them!

If you see this version of the icon, check that any hardware switch for your wireless connection is turned on. On some laptops, this is an easy switch to turn off accidentally. (See below, 'Physical switches and wireless access'.)

If the switch is on, and you still see a red X through the icon, then it probably means that there are no wireless networks detectable from where you are. Either that, or your wireless circuitry is completely on the blink, but this is rare.

Physical switches and wireless access

One of the most useful switches you can have on a laptop is a physical on-off switch for wireless access. It's great for turning off the wireless circuitry to save a bit of power either when you don't have access, or don't need it. Its usefulness, however, doesn't mean it can't cause problems.

On my wife's laptop, the wireless access on-off switch is a small black plastic switch labelled with tiny raised black plastic letters on a black plastic background, all tucked underneath the left edge of the keyboard. If the machine is moved slightly, it's easy to flick the switch off without realising. We've spent many frustrating minutes trying to figure out why her wireless access has stopped working.

On my own laptop, the wireless access on-off switch is much more visible and useful; it's right on top of the keyboard above the function keys. It glows blue when it's on and yellow when it's off. Unlike my wife, I never turn the switch off by accident, but I sometimes turn it off on purpose, to save power when I'm running on batteries or when there are no wireless networks available.

Not connected – connections are available

 A yellow sunburst on the Network icon means there are networks available, but you're not yet connected. You usually don't see this when you're at home because your laptop automatically connects to your home network and simply shows bars to indicate signal strength, as described below.

If you see this at home it can mean your home network is unavailable. In my experience, this has two causes: my wife or I turned off the router at the wall to save energy, or my Internet provider has encountered a fault of some kind, which has interrupted the service. The first is easily fixed by turning the router back on. The second sends me on a frantic search for the telephone helpline number for my broadband service provider. (Perhaps I should take this as a cue to read some poetry, or do something else pleasant or constructive that doesn't require wireless access, but I don't.)

You'll frequently see this version of the icon when you're out and about with your laptop and would like to find an Internet connection if possible. In either scenario you'll want to look into your options.

Figure 9.1

To start your search, click the Network icon; a list of available wireless networks appears. Nowadays, if you live near other people, there are likely to be a number of networks available. There are four types of networks that you might find listed:

- Your own home wireless network that you usually use.

- Other people's home wireless networks.

- A school, organisation, café, city or other network that's intended for sharing. It might provide free for all access or there might be security key or password-protected for limited access; or there might be a fee. For instance, in a fitness club or pub, you might be given the password because you're a member, or customer. The access might also be time-limited.

- An open network that's specifically designed for paid access. This is common in airports and many other public locations. Access is often quite expensive, several pounds per hour. However, in the UK, BT has started a wireless network called BT OpenZone. Cost is intended to be low enough to compete with getting your own home broadband.

BT OpenZone can be a lifesaver if you're visiting a friend who doesn't have home wireless or if you're home and have a problem with your usual wireless access. I've used it both ways. It's a bit expensive for short-term access however, currently priced at about £6 for 90 minutes.

When you first choose a network from the list, a checkbox appears called 'Connect automatically'. The checkbox is ticked by default. Always untick this checkbox unless you're sure the network in question is one you want to use again and again. If you don't un-tick the checkbox, your laptop will try to connect to this network every time it's in range, which will use up power and cause you extra steps when your laptop attempts to connect.

No Internet access

Your laptop is trying to connect to a network, but needs a password, payment or some other step to be taken.

If there's a network available that you've previously used, or that you've just selected for connection, but it needs a password or payment, the Network icon will show a yellow exclamation point. When you mouse over it, the words appear: No Internet access.

A network security key is a specific kind of password that's requested by the router which provides the wireless connection for a wireless network. It must be 13 or 26 characters long, depending on the specific type of security in use. To connect to most home networks and some simple setups in businesses or public places, you enter the network security key directly.

This is confusing because you've just seen a list of one or more networks and selected one available. You would expect all that's required is to enter a password or payment information. Yet here you are being told 'No Internet access'.

What the message really means is that you do have a *connection*, but you don't have Internet *access* – yet. If your effort to log on is successful, though, you will in a moment.

Usually, to access the network in question, you open a web browser window. (This is not an obvious thing to do when you've just been told you have no Internet access!) The web browser automatically opens a web page showing the request for a password or payment. You enter the password or make the payment and are allowed onto the network.

You may already have opened a web page and seen a warning that it can't connect (which is what led you to look at the Networks icon and try to find a network to use.) Confusingly, if you select a network and are ready to enter a password or payment, the web page may still show its previous warning. Simply refresh the web page, which should allow you to enter your password or payment information.

Internet access

 What you want to see is the icon that shows Internet access. The icon shows five bars, which are empty or filled in depending on how strong the wireless signal is where you're located.

If you're quite close to the source of the wireless signal then you're likely to see four or five bars filled in; representing a full-strength signal.

If you have three or fewer bars, it usually means that you're either fairly far from the source of the wireless signal, or there are objects interfering with the signal between you and the source, or both. However, I've successfully connected and worked with just one bar filled in. If something else comes along to interfere, however – and this can be as simple a change as someone opening or closing a door – you may lose your connection. Don't worry about this until it happens.

Usually, having any bars filled means you can exchange email, surf the Web and so on with no problems. Sometimes, a very weak connection will allow you to exchange email, but not to surf the Web.

If you're at home, you may have access in some rooms and not others, depending on how far each room is from your home broadband router. Try moving around the house, testing how many bars you get in different places, and seeing where the connection fails completely. You may be able to extend the range of your wireless signal by moving the router just a few feet in one direction or another.

If you really want to work in a spot that's outside the range of your router, get in touch with your wireless broadband provider; you may be able to move the router to a more central location, or get a booster that will amplify the signal to additional areas of the house.

Getting to the list of networks

Sometimes the list of networks in the panel above the Networks icon in the Notifications area doesn't appear. Instead, you see a link, Open Network and Sharing Center. To see the list of icons from here, simply click the link. The Network and Sharing Center control panel appears. Click the link, Connect to a network, and the list of networks appears.

Just because it's possible to sign onto a network for free doesn't mean you should. A place-based network such as in a gym or café should be safe. However, should you just happen to come across a network that you can log onto without a password, be careful. Firstly, in all likelihood, the network will belong to the legitimate user who simply hasn't thought to secure it. Just as you wouldn't plug your TV into someone else's electricity supply, likewise, don't hop onto a wireless connection somebody else is paying for. Equally, however, it could belong to someone who waits for you to connect to their 'free' network, then attempts to access the information on your computer. Similarly, the person providing the network may have done so in an attempt to put a virus on your computer, just for 'fun'. So think twice before taking advantage of a seemingly 'free' network.

Step by step: finding a network and signing on

At home, your laptop should find your home network and connect to it automatically. If this doesn't happen, or if you're away from home, you may need to take extra steps to get connected.

If you're in a gym, pub, café or other environment with a place-based wireless network that you should be able to access, ask for the password. If not, search through available wireless networks looking for public access points.

In an airport, you'll almost certainly have access only to a paid network, usually at a fairly high price of several pounds per hour.

Here's a step-by-step description of how to proceed:

1. Check the Networks icon in the Notifications area of the Taskbar. If it shows a yellow starburst, hover the cursor over the icon; the words 'Not connected – connections are available' will appear. This means there are networks you may be able to connect to. If it shows a yellow exclamation mark, go to Step 3.

   If you open a web browser at this point, you'll see an error message showing that you have no Internet access.

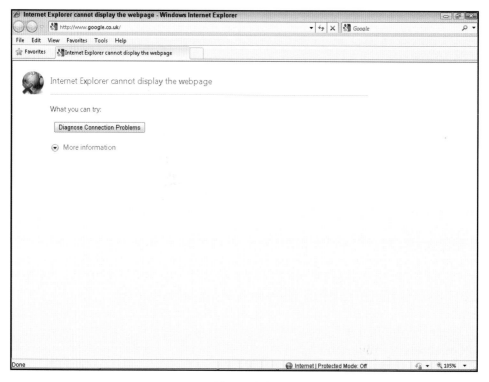

Figure 9.2

2. Click the Networks icon to see a list of available networks. Click the one you want to connect to; if a Connect button appears, and you believe the network to be safe, click the Connect button.

   You may be lucky enough to find a free public network available. If the network has no password protection, you may be allowed to connect. If it has password protection, you'll be asked for the password. If it's a paid-access network, you'll be asked to pay.

   If the network requires a password or payment, the Networks icon will change to show an exclamation mark.

3. With the Networks icon showing an exclamation point, open a web browser. If you already have a Web browser open, click Refresh.

   The web browser will show a request to enter a password, or a username and password. The specific look of the screen will vary depending on the setup where you're being asked to sign in.

Reproduced by permission of David Lloyd Leisure Ltd.

Figure 9.3

4. Enter the information,

Enter user names and passwords carefully. They're often deliberately designed to be hard to remember and therefore are easy to enter incorrectly.

5. With the Networks icon showing bars – meaning that you have a connection – check your web browser window.

   The web browser window should refresh and display a welcome message; it may also display advertisements. An additional, usually smaller browser window may open showing information about your connection. If your access has a time limit, the smaller browser window may show a countdown timer displaying the amount of time you have remaining for your connection.

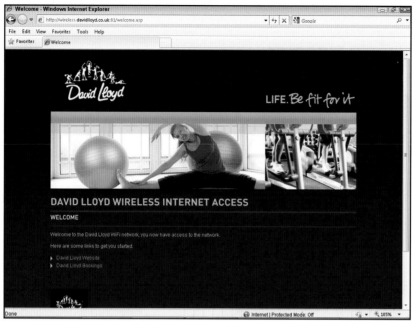

Reproduced by permission of David Lloyd Leisure Ltd.

Figure 9.4

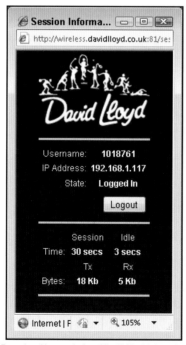

Reproduced by permission of David Lloyd Leisure Ltd.

Figure 9.5

Free wireless access everywhere?

When wireless networks first became available, many cities announced plans to provide free wireless access to all comers. Most of those plans have yet to be realised.

There are still some spots where people can access a network for free, but they're usually cafés, pubs and restaurants, where you're paying by being a customer. Some libraries and a few spots in various cities and towns are all that remain of the dream of free municipal Wi-Fi.

After many years of trying, planes are finally getting wireless Internet service, but expect to pay for it if it's available at all.

Using mobile broadband

Mobile broadband uses the mobile telephone network – the same network used by mobile phones – to provide you with access to the internet. You have a myriad of options when choosing a provider including O2, BT, Vodafone, 3 and many others. Each provides a similar service, but differs in pricing, coverage and the amount of data you are allowed to use. Luckily, there are several websites that can help you make sense of all the various options such as Broadband.co.uk's guide located at **http://www.broadband.co.uk/mobile-broadband/**.

Mobile broadband does not require the use of a landline, so it's a very good option for use while away from home. In fact, some use mobile broadband connections as their exclusive ISP. If you choose to go down this route, be sure you understand your data usage and pricing plan. Using more data than your allotment on a mobile broadband connection can be expensive.

If you use mobile broadband for your laptop you're likely to have a limit on how much data you can transfer per month for a fixed price, with additional data over the limit costing much more. However, to avoid the worry of a nasty surprise in the form of a large bill, contact your provider to find out how you can frequently check your usage.

If you select a mobile broadband package, you will be provided with a dongle – a small piece of hardware that may look like a USB memory stick. The dongle plugs into one of your laptop's USB ports and acts as the modem for the mobile broadband service. You are also likely to receive software, possibly in the form of a CD ROM, but more often on the dongle itself, that allows your laptop to communicate with the mobile network. If you are uncomfortable with installing your mobile software, this may be a perfect opportunity to have a cup of tea with your guardian angel.

Mobile broadband packages typically come in the following varieties:

● Pay As You Go – With a pay as you go plan, you generally purchase a dongle, which sometimes comes with some data usage. You can then add additional data usage by purchasing top ups. This works very much like pay as you go mobile phones. This type of mobile broadband plan is a good way to be sure you are not surprised by additional usage charges.

● Contract – With a contract, you are signing up to be charged monthly as you would with your home broadband. A typical mobile broadband contract is for 12 or 24 months and each month you are given a data usage allowance. If you use more than your allowance, you will incur additional charges. If you choose this option, you will be provided with an account website where you can check your usage, something I recommend to ensure you stay within your limits.

Mobile broadband is a good solution while you are out and about, especially if you are in an area where you do not have access to a wireless network or simply don't want to go to the trouble of searching for and accessing a wireless network. If mobile broadband appeals to you, I suggest you start with a pay as you go plan to get some experience in using mobile broadband, and to ensure you are not met with any nasty surprise charges.

Alternatives to a wireless network

Sometimes there are no wireless networks available. For those of us who are heavy laptop users, this is a minor tragedy. Without wireless access a big part of the fun you could have, or the work you could get done, using your laptop will either be impossible, or much harder and quite frustrating.

It's only when wireless access isn't available that you realise just how great it is. With wireless access you can use your computer, your programs, your saved files, plus email and the Web, wherever you happen to be. The combination is really powerful, which explains why laptops are now out-selling desktops.

Here are alternatives for online access when you can't get it through your laptop:

● Working without online access

● Using a borrowed computer, or a computer in an Internet café

● Using a mobile phone.

I'll explain each of these options here, plus a trick for getting the most out of computers in Internet cafés. Keep them in mind when you're out and about, with or without your computer.

The memory stick trick

Two of the best wheezes I've come across throughout my computer experience relate to two fairly new advances:

● Windows 7's separation of your personal data files into separate folders: documents, pictures, music and videos.

● The availability of affordable USB 'memory sticks'

The trick is to regularly copy your documents folder – which, for me, has mostly Word files, saved web pages and a few spreadsheets – onto a 2GB memory stick whenever you go out. This way, you can go to an Internet café and always have your most important personal files with you.

USB memory sticks come in all sorts of shapes and sizes now, and even a very large 8GB drive, which cost about £50 in 2008, is now available for well under £20.

The Internet café I use most often has USB connectors right on the desktop; I don't have to bend down to plug my memory stick into the machine itself. I'm able to edit my current documents or save interesting web pages for reference.

I then copy the My Documents Folder file back and forth to the memory stick. This can be tricky, and there is a risk of losing your most recent files or changes if you click the wrong button. However, it's worth it to have a recent backup and to have up-to-date copies of your files wherever you go.

Working without online access

You can get more done when you don't have online access by doing a little extra work when you do have it. Here are a few things I've learned to do:

- **Do research at home**. Before I go out to some place where I might not have Internet access, I do any online research I might need. For instance, if I'm going to be writing a letter to a friend, I might check the weather where they are or look up flight information for a future visit before I go out. Then I have the information I need for writing the letter at hand.

- **Put an 'out of office' message on email**. Various email packages, including the two email tools I use regularly – Google Mail and Microsoft Outlook – have the capacity to send an 'out of office' reply to emails that are sent to you. You can include your mobile phone number in the 'out of office' reply if you want people to use it, or just give a timeframe in which you'll be able to reply. It's fine to say 'tomorrow', or some date even further in the future; as long as you set expectations the way you want to, no one will be concerned.

- **Email files back and forth.** When I don't bother with the memory stick trick described above, I email files back and forth to myself so I have them handy. This is great in an Internet café, but doesn't work very well on mobile phones, even the ones that can access attached files.

- **Use a mobile phone for email**. I can use my mobile phone to quickly check my email. It's no good for typing long replies, but at least I know if anyone's trying to reach me, and I can send a brief reply by email, text or a phone call. (Once you have a laptop, and especially if you keep in regular email contact with people, a phone with email access capability could become an increasing necessity for this reason alone).

- **Use a mobile phone for web pages**. I can quickly check the address of a doctor's office, say, on the Web using my phone. This can be a hassle, and research shows that people are much less effective at completing tasks on the Web using a phone than with a laptop or desktop computer. However, in a pinch, Web access from your phone is better than nothing.

None of this is great; I can't access my laptop files from a mobile, nor save an interesting web page to my laptop from it. There's a reason people are so quick to connect to the Internet access on their laptops whenever they can, even when it costs them aggravation, money and battery life. Having workarounds, however, even if they're not quite as good, can make things a lot easier.

I've taken the use of substitutes to extremes. I've written two books 'on the move'. I'm not the first, and I won't be the last; the famous author John Grisham wrote his first best-seller on his laptop whilst on the train back and forth to his job as a lawyer in Chicago.

For my first book, when I had a fairly long commute by train, I brought my laptop. It was a bother, but I got quite a bit done. I learned to do research at home, before or after travelling, and to put notes in the manuscript to indicate where I needed to go back and look for something else.

For the second book, when I had a similar length commute on the London Underground and couldn't count on having a seat, I used a Blackberry mobile phone. Blackberries have little keyboards that you type on with your thumbs. I was worried at first that I'd be wasting time, but I tested myself, and my typing speed on the Blackberry was about half my speed on a proper keyboard. I realised that even for a 50,000 word book, I'd only spend about 15 extra hours typing on the Blackberry out of the weeks of work the writing would take me. I wrote the first draft on the Blackberry and later drafts on my laptop. I've since heard that I'm not the only one to have done this.

Using an Internet café

You might think that getting a laptop and home broadband means you'd never need to go in an Internet café. The opposite is true, however. Once you get used to doing things on a computer and having Internet access, it's hard to live without it for long.

An Internet café is different to a café with Internet access. An Internet café has PCs – usually Windows PCs only – that are available for customer use, usually by the hour or half hour. In better establishments, each PC has a web cam, headphones with a microphone and a flexible USB port to make most of the things you'd want to do easy. Some even have small cubicles for privacy during voice or video calls.

Internet cafés are great. For about a pound an hour you can do most of the things you want to do on a computer. A good Internet café has Windows, Microsoft Office and rock-solid Internet access on every machine. If you carry your files on a memory stick, email them to yourself; or simply do a good job of integrating new work with old when you get back to your laptop.

Internet cafés aren't only great for longer sessions. They're also excellent for quickly checking your email. I've been at an Internet café five minutes before closing time when someone came in the door and begged to be allowed onto a computer just for a few minutes to check for an email. He was granted the privilege and cheerfully paid the minimum charge of 50p, which would normally have bought him half an hour's time online, just for those few minutes.

An Internet café can be a good alternative to bringing your laptop on holiday. If you settle someplace for a week or two, it might be worthwhile to bring your laptop. If you're on the move a lot, though, you might prefer to leave the laptop behind and drop friends and family an email from an Internet café during your trip.

You can look up Internet cafés at a site called **www.easyinternetcafe.com.** This used to be the home of the Easy group's own Internet cafés, but is now an online search site for all Internet cafés worldwide.

Reproduced from easyinternetccafe.com

Figure 9.6

Summary

- Staying connected to the Internet whenever possible is vital for getting the most out of your laptop.

- When you take your laptop out of the house, staying connected becomes more difficult. Many laptop users have favourite haunts where they know they can get connected, such as a library, café, pub or gym with wireless Internet access.

- Finding and choosing a wireless network can be confusing at first but becomes easier with practice.

Brain Training

There may be more than one correct answer to these questions.

1. Where is it easiest for most laptop users to stay connected?

a) At home

b) In restaurants

c) In shopping centres

d) On a plane

2. Which icon means 'this laptop is online'?

a) A red X over bars

b) A sunburst over bars

c) A yellow exclamation point over bars

d) One or more bars filled in

3. What should you check if you suddenly lose access at home?

a) That there's no aluminium foil in the vicinity

b) That the wireless access switch on your laptop is on

c) That your television volume is not turned up too high

d) That your router is turned on

4. Where do you check first for a wireless network?

a) The Start button

b) Google

c) The Sharing control panel

d) The Network icon

Answers

Q1 – a   **Q2** – d   **Q3** – b and d   **Q4** – d

Using your laptop's software

10

Equipment needed: a laptop

Skills needed: some knowledge of the keyboard, mouse and operating system to try built-in programs.

One of the most daunting sights for a novice laptop user is the initial Start menu in Windows or, to a lesser extent, the Dock on a Mac. The applications, utilities and data files listed may appear confusing and quite overwhelming. Where on Earth does one begin?

In this chapter I'll show you how to do a few essential things with your computer. In demonstrating these simple tasks, the process will be de-mystified and you'll begin to feel confident using the Start menu and a few of the tools on it. Once you've used some of the resources, you will come to view the Start menu or Mac Dock as a toolbox full of interesting and useful tools.

In this chapter I'll start by showing you how to use a couple of built-in utilities for running your system. I'll then take you through the steps for creating and editing a simple word processing document, followed by a spreadsheet.

In this book, I emphasise programs and functions that are likely to be available not only on your own laptop but on computers in Internet cafés, in the homes of friends and family and so on. This gives you maximum flexibility in using both your own laptop and other computers when you have to.

This chapter focuses on things you can do without having to be online. Understanding how to use the software on your computer when you're offline builds a base for taking full advantage of online resources as well.

It's quite common, when on the move with your laptop, to be offline part of the time. You need to know how to get the best out of both.

By going through some simple exercises using the built-in functions of your computer, as shown in this chapter, you'll familiarise yourself with many of its fundamental capabilities. You'll then feel more equipped to get the most out of your online experience, which I'll introduce in the next chapter.

Scratching the surface

You can do much more with your laptop than described here, of course. Over time, you might consider exploring all the software on your laptop to understand everything you have available and when you might need it.

You can also extend your laptop's capabilities by connecting it to various hardware. Mobile phones, digital cameras and video cameras are just a few of the devices you can usefully plug into your computer.

No matter how you end up using your laptop, getting to grips with the basics described here will prove invaluable.

Using Accessories

The Accessories folder in the Windows All Programs folder holds what are often called 'utilities' – small, simple programs that do small, simple jobs. These small tasks are often very important.

To see the programs in the Accessories folder, click Start, choose All Programs, then click the Accessories folder.

In addition to the programs at the top level of Accessories, there are several sub-level folders with additional programs. In particular, look at the tools in the System Tools folder and the Ease of Access folder, which I describe in more detail below.

Figure 10.1

Here are the Accessories programs you are most likely to need, day in and day out:

- **Calculator**. Does what it says on the tin. Replacement Calculator programs that do more, look better and so on are popular free, or even paid, downloads. You may want to visit CNET's popular website, **www.download.com**, and see if you can find one you like. Look up 'maths calculator' to narrow the search to replacements for the built-in Windows calculator.

- **Notepad**. This is the simplest possible text editing program.

If you're working unplugged and are desperate to save battery life, running Notepad or WordPad instead of full-featured word processor programs will probably extend your battery life by a few minutes.

- **Paint**. I love this program! It's a very simple graphics capture and editing program.

- **WordPad**. WordPad is the simplest word processing program, with basic formatting capability such as **bold** and *italics*.

Be very careful about downloading programs to your computer. Some programs can steal your personal information and send it to criminals or do all sorts of other nasty things. Programs on Download.com are carefully checked for viruses and are usually safe to download and run.

Why are so many important programs buried in folders and sub-folders? People who are new to computers often wonder why the programs they need most are so hard to find. The answer is that Windows isn't that different from your house. At any given time, you might need a fork, or a two-year-old tax return, or your passport. In between such times, however, you have to store them somewhere. Just as you know the whereabouts of these different items in your house, the same is true with Windows. You simply need to learn your way around. Once you gain a bit of knowledge and confidence, you'll be able to find what you need, when you need it.

Adding sums on the Calculator

To get you comfortable with using Accessories programs, I'll walk you through using a simple program that does something quite familiar, the Calculator.

Figure 10.2

You may be tempted to pick up an actual calculator when you need to calculate a sum. If your laptop is up and running, I encourage you to use the one on your computer instead. Why? Mainly because it's good practice. You can also move on from the calculator to a word processing program to save the result, or to a spreadsheet to do more calculating.

Let's start the Calculator, do a simple calculation, then close it again:

Here's a step-by-step description of how to proceed:

1. Click the Start button.

   The Start menu appears.

2. Click All Programs.

   A list of the programs on your computer appears.

3. Use the scroll bar in the All Programs list, if needed, to view the Accessories folder.

   Scrolling within a menu requires some co-ordination to do smoothly; if you're new to computers, it may take you a couple of tries to do it right. Don't worry – it may be a bit fiddly at first, but will quickly become second nature after a little practice.

4. Click the Accessories folder.

   A list of the Accessories programs on your computer appears.

5. Click Calculator. You can either click the little icon, on the word Calculator, or anywhere on the line on which the icon and the word appear.

   The Calculator opens.

6. In the Calculator, click Help.

   The Help menu opens.

7. Click View Help.

   Windows searches online for the latest Help content. If an Internet connection is available, an up-to-the-minute version of the Help content appears. If no Internet connection is available, a stored version appears. Read the Help if you're interested in learning more about how the Calculator works.

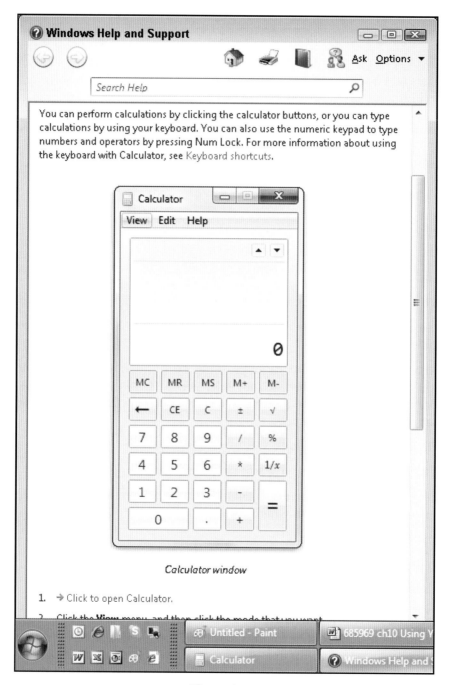

Calculator window

8. Try entering a simple calculation. For instance, if the current rate of VAT is 15%, you can find out the pre-tax price of a £93 product that has had VAT applied by entering the following formula: 93/1.15=.

   The answer – approximately 80.87, for the problem given here – will appear in the display area.

9. To copy the result, click Edit at the top of the Calculator, then click Copy from the menu that appears.

   The currently displayed result is copied into the Windows Clipboard.

The Windows Clipboard is a hidden area that holds information between the time you copy it, as you have just done here, and when you paste it elsewhere. The Clipboard is available in most Windows programs.

10. On the Calculator, click the C button to clear the result.

    A value of 0 will appear in the calculator's display area.

11. To paste the previous result, click Edit at the top of the Calculator, then click Paste from the menu that appears.

    The information you previously copied to the Windows clipboard is pasted into the calculator's display area. This demonstrates, in a simple way, how copy and paste works.

12. To see everything this 'simple' calculator can do, click the View menu.

    A list of different types of calculators appears. You have access to several types: Standard, Scientific, Programmer and Statistics. Use the one that best suits your needs.

To learn more about the Clipboard, look it up in Windows Help. Click Start ⇨ Help and Support, then enter Clipboard in the search box.

Saving a screenshot

We all get stuck sometimes, but not many of us have in-house technical support when using our laptop. The natural thing to do at this point is to call someone; to 'phone a friend', as they say on the TV game show 'Who Wants to be a Millionaire'?

It can be rather difficult to help someone with their computer over the phone, when they can't see what's wrong onscreen.

One of the best ways to work around this is to learn how to capture a screenshot of what's currently on your computer screen and email it to someone. This can save huge amounts of time and frustration for all concerned.

Screenshots are also great for sharing fun and interesting things with other people. While there are a lot of ways to save information from your computer, capturing what's onscreen is almost always a straightforward way to do it.

To create a screenshot you use the Windows clipboard, mentioned in the previous set of steps, and the Accessories program, Paint. You can then send the file as an attachment to an email message. I'll discuss email in some detail in the next chapter.

The steps below can be a bit tricky. Much of this is the unavoidable result of cramming a lot of functionality into a laptop along with subsequent, gradual improvements over time. Hang in there; with a little practice, you'll soon become familiar with the little complexities and nuances.

Follow these steps to copy a screenshot:

1. To copy the whole screen to the Clipboard, press the Print Screen key. (The key may be labelled prt sc, Prt Scn or a similar label). You may need to hold down the Function key, usually labelled fn, for Print Screen to work. If so, the label prt sc may be in a box, and the Function key label, fn, may be in a box as well, to show that they work together.

    Sorry this is so complicated, but space on laptop keyboards is at a premium, as is space on the keys themselves, so labels tend to be compressed.

    Once you press Print Screen successfully, the current contents of your screen will be copied to the Windows Clipboard. The Clipboard is described in the previous section.

2. Open Windows Paint: click Start ⇨ All Programs ⇨ Accessories ⇨ Paint.

   Windows Paint opens.

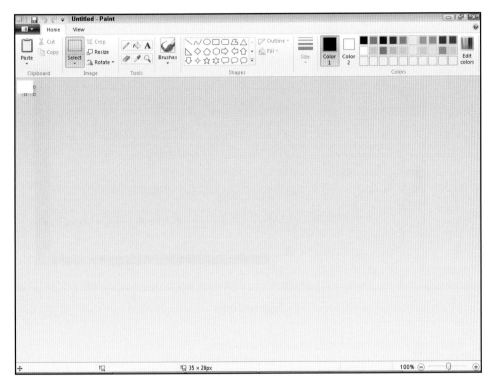

Figure 10.4

3. Press Ctrl+V to paste the clipboard contents into Windows Paint. (You can also click the Home tab and choose Clipboard ⇨ Paste.)

   The screen image is copied into Windows Paint. Note the Paint program window information at the top of the screen to help orient yourself to what's going on.

4. Open the Paint menu. Hover the mouse over the little icon that looks like a list in the upper left of the window; the word Paint appears; click the icon. Alternatively, use the keyboard to enter Alt+F to open the menu.

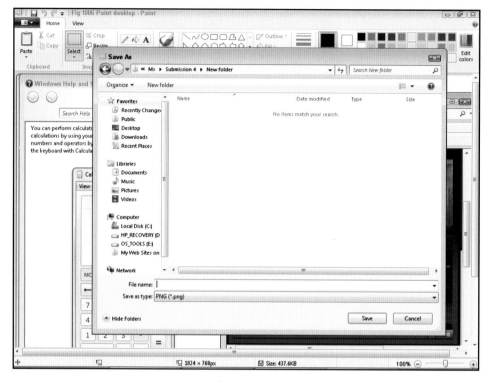

Figure 10.5

5. From the Paint/File menu, choose Save As.

    The Save As dialogue will open.

6. Choose a location in which to save the file. For simplicity's sake, in the area in the left-hand side of the dialogue, click the icon, Desktop.

    The Windows Desktop is now the selected destination for your file.

7. From the pull-down menu near the bottom of the dialogue, called Save as type, choose PNG.

    PNG is a type of graphics file that combines an accurate image with a relatively small file size.

 Getting in the habit of choosing the type of file before entering the file name may save you a lot of trouble with your files in the future.

8. Next to the prompt, File name, enter a file name. Enter any name you like, but a short file name, about 15 characters or fewer, will be easier to view in various lists in Windows.

Don't include a full stop in the file name; Windows will let you do it, but you may end up confusing yourself, and there's even a chance you'll confuse Windows. Windows tends to treat letters after a full stop as a file type, so if you have a full stop followed by letters that are the same as a file type, then accidentally erase the actual file type, Windows could get confused.

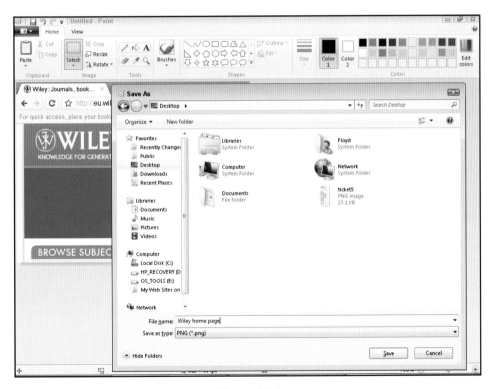

Figure 10.6

9. Click Save.

The file will be saved to the desktop.

I've taken to including the file type in the name of graphics files to make it easier to find just the file version I need. For instance, I'd name a file like this one something like 'Screen capture PNG'.

10. To verify that the file saved correctly, hover the cursor over the little strip in the lower right-hand corner of your screen.

    The words Show desktop appear.

11. Click the Show desktop button.

    The desktop appears, with the icon for the file you just saved on the desktop.

12. Hover the cursor over the icon for the file you just created.

    A description of the file will appear.

13. Double-click the icon for the file you just created.

    The file will open in Windows Picture Viewer.

To open the file in Paint instead of Windows Picture Viewer, right-click on the icon instead of double-clicking it. From the context-sensitive menu that appears, choose Open with, then choose Paint from the list of programs that appears.

14. Click the red X in the upper right corner to close Windows Picture Viewer.

    Windows Picture Viewer closes.

    Congratulations! You've saved your first screenshot. This is a great technique to use should you run into problems, so it's good to practise this early on.

You can also save the front most, active window from the screen, rather than the full screen. This makes the file smaller and easier to identify exactly what you want to show someone. Just hold down the Alt key while choosing Print Screen. (On some systems, you'll have to hold down the Function key to select Print Screen, then hold down Alt in addition.)

continued

When the file is open in Paint, you can highlight certain things by drawing a red circle around them, etc.

To get experience with these options, try them now. Follow the steps above, but press Alt when capturing the screen image, and try different tools in Paint to add a red arrow or circle or box to highlight areas of interest.

Graphics file formats

There are many ways to save graphics files on computers. If you save a very accurate image, it can take up a lot of memory and be slow to transmit over the Internet. If you compress the image to save space, you can create a smaller file that you can send over the Internet faster, but at the expense of loss of quality in the image.

Screenshots, even from a large screen, are considered quite simple files from a graphics point of view. The best way to save them these days is as a PNG file. PNG files are a newer type of file format than the older Internet-supported file types, GIF and JPEG. These days, you should use PNG for most graphics images and JPEG for photographs.

Windows 7 includes another tool in the Accessories area, called the Snipping Tool that serves a similar purpose to doing a screen capture. However, the Snipping Tool is not available on all Windows computers, as is the combination of the Print Screen key, the Windows Clipboard and Paint. However, try the Snipping Tool if you think it might be a good addition to your bag of tricks.

Using Ease of Access Tools

Windows includes an Ease of Access centre and ease of access tools in every computer. These are beginning versions of tools for people who just need a bit of help or are working on an unfamiliar computer. If you have serious difficulties using a computer, there are specialist tools that can help you. Check with disabilities organisations and agencies in your area for more help. The Royal

National Institute of the Blind can serve as a good first point of call right across the UK. You can find them on the Web at **www.rnib.org**.

If you have a disability, the easiest way to get started with these tools is to have an experienced computer user help you. That way you can readily try different tools and begin to develop a working style that's most effective for you. Once you have things set up properly and have learned the tools you need, you can work independently. However, if you're patient, there's nothing to stop you trying the tools on your own as well.

The Ease of Access Centre includes:

- **Magnifier**. The magnifier shows parts of the screen zoomed in, to help if you have visual problems. This works especially well with a separate monitor connected to your laptop. That way you can have a standard-resolution desktop on the laptop and put zoomed-in highlights on the separate screen. When you're on the move, with no additional screen, you can have standard resolution on half your laptop's screen and the zoomed-in part over to the side.

- **Narrator**. This tool reads out text on the screen aloud. This is a good tool for those who have trouble viewing detail, but it takes practice to use effectively.

- **High Contrast**. This is a quick tool for changing the colours onscreen to increase contrast for people with different types of vision problems.

- **On-Screen Keyboard**. Using a keyboard can be tough for people with various physical disabilities. The on-screen keyboard allows you to type by using a mouse, which many people find easier to control.

Using word processing and spreadsheets

Word processing allows you to use your computer as a super-typewriter and publishing tool. Spreadsheets allow you to manipulate numbers and other data.

Here, I'll guide you through a simple word processing tool and a full-featured spreadsheet. You can learn how to do basic or intermediate word processing on your own, plus some spreadsheet essentials.

Spreadsheets, though, are a little more complex. Get the basics firmly under your belt before trying out the more advanced tasks. You may, of course, be one of

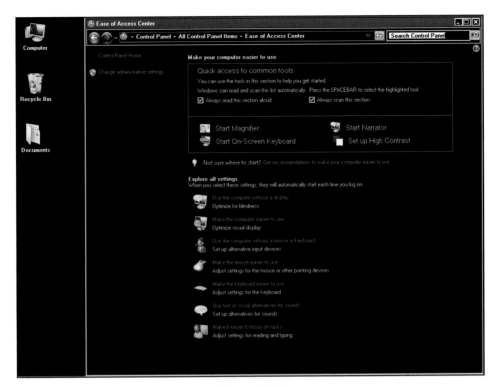

Figure 10.7

those lucky people who gets the hang of spreadsheets quickly. In that case, just proceed at your own pace.

For most people, though, more in-depth training is needed to learn to use spreadsheets – whether from a patient friend or family member, in a class or from a book. With a little proficiency, you can use spreadsheets to do amazing things, from your taxes to running a business, including creating some striking charts and graphics.

Although it is beyond the scope of this book to go into any detail, there are two other major categories of traditional software you will find it useful to know about.

The first is presentation programs. The best known and widely-used presentation program for Windows is called Microsoft PowerPoint. It's included in even the most basic versions of Microsoft Office.

PowerPoint makes it easy to create full-screen, full-page charts called slides. Each is usually a mix of up to 25 or so words and a graphic or two. Presentations are popular demonstration and promotional tools.

Figure 10.8

It's easy to find PowerPoint presentations online; for instance, companies often use this format to release their annual financial reports. If you want to get a feel for how presentations are used, look up PowerPoint in a search engine. You're likely to come across any number of presentations that demonstrate the software's functionality and which may be of interest.

The other major category of software is called databases, which store and process information. Your driver's license information, for instance, is stored on a database maintained by the government.

Many people use spreadsheets for storing information, but a proper database gives a lot more control over how information is stored and retrieved. The most popular database for personal use is called Microsoft Access. It's included in more expensive business and advanced versions of Microsoft Office, not in the basic version most people have for home use.

Creating a simple word processing document

When not online, computer users probably spend more time word processing than any other computer function. We love words, and word processing allows us to do all sorts of things with them.

As a laptop user, it's good to know how to get the most out of simple word processing tools that use up less screen space, fewer computer resources and, when you're not connected to power, less of your battery's capacity.

In the example here, I'll use WordPad. It's particularly appropriate for laptop users as it's simpler, and may use less power when you're running on batteries, than a comprehensive package like Microsoft Word. You can also use Notepad, which is even simpler, to save a bit more power when you don't need any formatting at all. Use Word to work on existing Word documents and when you need more functionality.

Follow these steps to create a simple word processing document:

1. Open WordPad. Choose Start ⇨ All Programs ⇨ Accessories ⇨ WordPad.

    WordPad opens.

2. Hover the cursor over various commands and buttons to see an explanation of what they do.

    Don't expect to memorise commands right away; just start to connect the images with an idea of what these commands actually do when you use them.

3. Enter some text – for instance, the first several lines of a letter to a friend or family member.

    Be sure to include several carriage returns, indicated by the down-and-left or Return key on your keyboard. This is because your word processor treats text separated by carriage returns as separate paragraphs.

4. Select individual characters and words by clicking and dragging. Change the font, bold, italics and other characteristics of individual letters by using the Font commands in WordPad.

You'll see the formatting change as you choose different options.

5. Triple-click to select a whole paragraph. (You may need to practice a bit to get this right; when you do, all the text between two places where you hit Return will be selected, marked by white on black display.) Change the indentation, bullets, and left, right or centre alignment to see the results.

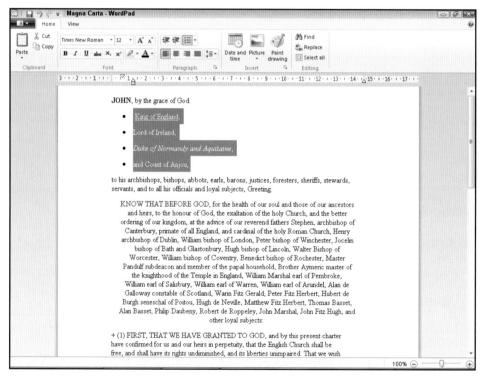

Figure 10.9

6. Practise saving, finding and retrieving documents.

To preserve formatting, save the document in Rich Text Format (RTF for short). Rich Text Format documents preserve all the formatting you can choose in WordPad and much, but not all, of the formatting you can use in Microsoft Word.

7. Practise saving files in different folders and finding them.

   A common frustration when using a computer is not being able to find a document you created or viewed previously. Guard against this by practising different ways of saving, naming and finding documents.

8. Save your file and close WordPad.

   You can improve your word processing skills through further experimentation in WordPad, Microsoft Word or another program, as well as by asking a friend to help, buying a book or taking a class.

If all you're running on a laptop is a word processing window or two, you can save a small amount of power by making the desktop background black. Right-click on the desktop and choose Personalize. Click the Desktop Background button and choose Solid Colors from the pull-down menu. Choose black as the background colour if you want to minimise power usage. Also, right-click on the taskbar, choose Properties, and then click in the checkbox to select Auto-hide the taskbar. This gives you more black background and more power savings. Then turn down your screen brightness to the lowest practical level for the lighting where you're working. I've used all these tricks to stretch my battery life to the maximum when I don't have access to mains power.

Creating a simple spreadsheet

In this section I'll demonstrate how to use a computer spreadsheet to enter a few items of data and get a total and an average.

The steps here assume you have Microsoft Office installed, including Microsoft Excel. If you have another spreadsheet installed, such as Microsoft Works, you can use that instead. Google has a simple spreadsheet program in Google Docs. You can try it at **www.docs.google.com**. Or you can use a computer in an Internet café with Microsoft Excel or Microsoft Works installed.

Follow these steps to create a simple spreadsheet:

1. Open Microsoft Excel (or other spreadsheet). Choose Start ➪ All Programs ➪ Office ➪ Microsoft Excel.

   Excel opens.

2. Put the cursor in the upper-left corner of the spreadsheet, which is called cell A1 (column A, row 1). Enter the word MONTH, in all capital letters.

3. Now, in the next cell over, called B1, enter the words INCHES OF RAIN.

    This will represent the rainfall in your area.

4. In cell A2, just under MONTH, enter the word January. Below it, enter February. Below that, enter March.

    Now it's time for some Excel magic.

5. Click January with the mouse and drag down to March to select these three cells.

    A box will appear around the cells.

6. Drag the right lower corner of the box down in column A until you reach row 13.

    The cells will automatically fill with the names of the remaining months of the year.

    Now that the month names are entered, it's time to enter some number values against them.

Excel can do this 'dragging' trick with many different types of dates and other values. You can enter the month names by their first three letters – Jan, Feb, Mar – and Excel will fill in the remaining cells with month names in the same style. You can add a year number and Excel will continue the year up to December, then start with January of the following year.

7. Enter a number in column B next to each of the month names.

    I suggest one-digit values between, say, 0 and 6. You might even think about it a bit and enter realistic values for the rainfall in your area each month.

8. Now, in cell A14, enter the word Total. In cell A15, enter the word Average.

    These words are labels for the values that will soon appear next to them. Next is the fun part.

9. Put the cursor in cell B14 and click the AutoSum button at the top of the window.

The Autosum button looks like this: Σ. When you click it, the cell will automatically fill in with a formula summarising the values above.

If you can't find the Autosum button, enter the formula directly:

=SUM(B2:B13)

The sum of the numbers you entered will appear in the cell.

10. Put the cursor in cell B15 and enter the following formula:

=AVERAGE(B2:B13).

The average of the numbers you entered will appear in the cell.

Now let's create a chart.

11. Select the month names and the values by clicking and dragging from cell A2 to cell B13.

The month names and the values next to them will be highlighted.

12. Click the Chart Wizard button.

The Chart Wizard will appear.

13. Select all the default values for the chart by clicking Next three times, then Finish.

A chart will appear in your spreadsheet showing the months and the value for each month.

14. Save the file, if you wish, and close Excel.

As you can imagine, there are many more things you can do with this program. However, this brief example shows off a great deal of Excel's functionality.

If you wish, you can use the simple example here to probe deeper into Excel's capability. For instance, try these additional steps:

● Underline the words Month and Rainfall, Total and Average, to distinguish them from the data labels. You can select all four cells at once by holding down the Control key, labelled ctrl (or similar) on your keyboard, then clicking each of the four cells in turn. Right-click on one of the cells, choose Format Cells from the cursor menu, choose the Font tab and single underlining. Click OK and the cells will change.

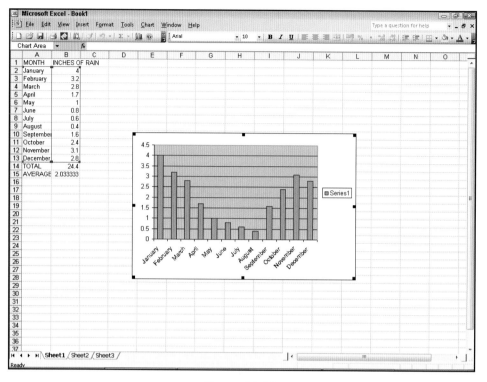

Figure 10.10

● Change the formatting of the number for the Average. Right-click on the value next to the word Average. Choose Format Cells and the tab, Number. Choose Number as the category and change the value, Decimal places, to 1. Click OK and the cell will change.

● Do more with the chart. Go through the process of creating the chart again and give it a title and other improvements. Once you have the chart, click it; little boxes that serve as handles will appear on the corners and edges. Grab a handle and stretch the chart onscreen with the mouse until all the month names appear in full. Double-click on the bars of the chart to bring up the Format Data Series dialogue and change their colour.

You can spend hours just changing the appearance of a spreadsheet or a chart. Once you get it the way you want it, the sense of achievement is very gratifying.

You don't need to be online to work on a spreadsheet, though you may gather your initial facts online. Once you have your data, however, you can work on a spreadsheet without any Internet connection necessary.

Summary

- Your laptop has a great deal of in-built software that you can use.
- In-built software can be used in a way that helps preserves battery life.
- Ease of Access tools can be helpful for people with disabilities.
- Saving a screenshot can be a useful way of communicating to others the difficulties you may encounter when using your computer.
- Spreadsheet programs are powerful, multi-faceted tools.

Brain Training

There may be more than one correct answer to these questions.

1. Where will you find Accessories programs in Windows?

a) On the desktop

b) In a folder in the All programs area of the Start menu

c) In the Taskbar

d) At the top level of the Start menu

2. Which of the following Accessories are on all Windows PCs?

a) Calculator

b) Multi-user dungeons (MUDs)

c) Notepad

d) Paint

3. What Accessory is best for capturing a screenshot?

a) Calculator

b) Multi-user dungeons (MUDs)

c) Notepad

d) Paint

4. Which tools are found in the Ease of Access Center?

a) Magnifier

b) Narrator

c) High Contrast

d) On-Screen Keyboard

Answers

Q1 – b   **Q2** – a, c and d   **Q3** – d   **Q4** – all of them

Learning what you can do online

11

Equipment needed: A laptop with wireless Internet access (see Chapter 9).

Skills needed: some knowledge of the keyboard, mouse and operating system to set up email access and use online capabilities.

The emergence of the World Wide Web is one of the most exciting stories of the last 20 years. The early days saw people using America Online (AOL) and Earthlink for email and for getting online via their home phone lines. The dot-com boom of the late 1990s swiftly followed, as did the subsequent bust in 2001. In today's world we have fast broadband access, online shopping as a commonplace activity, free phone calls through your computer, YouTube for videos, Facebook for communicating with friends and family, and Twitter for sending and receiving short messages.

The possibilities are endless, and the choices can seem more than a little overwhelming if you're not used to spending time online. In this chapter I'll introduce a few of the top websites and how you can use them to get up and running on the Web.

The sites in this chapter are among the biggest and most popular in the world. The tasks shown here are things most regular Web users would already be familiar with. You should become comfortable with the activities described to help prepare you for your own explorations later on. Having thoroughly investigated on your own, you'll feel more confident when others give you suggestions and advice.

There are certain factors you should be aware of when online, both in terms of protecting your personal information and your actual computer itself. Similarly, there are websites out there containing extreme and/or offensive material which you will certainly want to avoid. The next chapter describes in detail how to protect yourself online. The sites I describe in this chapter are all quite safe. Stick to these sites and other 'name' sites at least until after you have read the next chapter.

Any brief survey of the Web will naturally be fairly generalised rather than covering the entire Web. There's simply too much there to cover completely. However, the sites described here are very popular and a good introduction to the range available out there.

Using email

Email may be the main thing that attracts most people to getting a laptop or other type of computer. Nowadays, everything seems to happen by email.

If you don't have email access, you could feel cut off from communication with friends, family, former work colleagues and others. Even banks, insurance companies and the Government want you to receive email from them and have you visit various websites.

One of the primary reasons people decide to get a laptop, rather than a desktop computer, is for on-the-go access to your email. Your laptop is not only great for helping you get online to send and receive email; being your familiar computing environment, with all your own programs and files stored there, your information and documents can be easily accessed or attached to emails whenever needed.

Seemingly constant email connection is a modern day phenomenon. We safely assume that everyone is logging into their emails at least once, if not several times per day. To support this need for constant connection, people now carry their laptops everywhere, sign on for expensive wireless connections at airports and so on, just to stay connected whenever possible.

Consequently, email is now, in some ways, less effective than it used to be. People receive so much email that they can't possibly reply to all of them. Important messages (such as those to your friends) can get lost among advertisements, online newsletters and other stuff.

What tends to happen is that high-priority messages that have to be answered right away do get an answer. Subsequently, other equally important communication, which doesn't fall into the 'right now' urgent category, like keeping up with a friend or family member, can, if we're not careful, remain unanswered indefinitely.

To help prevent this happening, you might want to keep track of the messages you send and follow up with a reminder after a few days. Find the message you sent and send it to the same person again with a brief note on top. That keeps your message popping up to the top of your correspondent's inbox. Most email programs, such as Microsoft Outlook (computer based) and Yahoo (web based) also allow you to 'flag' an email for follow up at a later date. This is usually represented by a small flag icon.

We'll now look at the kinds of email accounts available and how to use Microsoft Outlook to manage email.

What kind of email account is best?

Email accounts are very cheap and easy for organisations to provide. That means it's easy to get several email accounts if you wish.

Email accounts have two parts. The first comprises a user name, which you choose. The second part takes the name of the provider supplying the email account.

For years I used an email account from Compuserve, an early provider of online access:

budsmith2000@compuserve.com

I couldn't just use 'budsmith' as my user name, as that had already been taken. I added the '2000' to make the name different and because I thought it sounded cool. Of course, I created that account at a time when the year 2000 was still a few years off in the future! I abandoned it years ago.

You'll probably get an email address from the provider of your home broadband. A lot of people in the UK have email addresses like this one:

budsmith2000@bt.com

If you have a mobile phone, you may also be given an email address from your mobile phone provider.

The trouble is, you may well want to change your broadband or mobile phone provider for a better deal later. Even if you stick with your provider, they may not offer an email service that has all the features you want. So you don't want to be stuck with the email address that provider gave you.

Once you start using the email address, however, you may find it hard to change. People may be used to contacting you at 'your' email address. You may also be on mailing lists for different email newsletters and even online bill-paying, with your bank, insurance company and more. You would need to notify all your contacts that you are now using a different email address. Similarly, you would need to update your email account details held on any websites you have signed up to. If possible, you might want to retain your old email address until the new one has 'stuck', just to make sure you don't lose any potentially important communication.

AOL was a very popular Internet Service Provider (ISP) all through the 1990s, when people tended to dial up over a phone line to get connected to the Internet. As people switched to broadband around 2000 and after, AOL fell behind. Yet today, years later, many people still keep their AOL account just because of the value of their '**@aol.com**' email address.

Before you start using an email address, try to make sure it's the one you want to use long-term.

Imagine if your real mail was delivered to several different addresses. (A common occurrence for any of us who have moved house!) You'd certainly get tired of 'going around the houses' to find your mail!

It's the same with email accounts. Although it's by no means set in stone that once you have set up an email account, you must stick with it forever, it does make practical sense for you to choose an email address and provider you intend to use for a while. That said, it's a competitive market, and in a bid to entice people to switch over to them, providers regularly update their services and functionality. It may be inevitable therefore, that at some stage, you find you may want to swap.

The most flexible kind of email account to use is what's called a 'Webmail' account. This is a web-based email account that is usually accessed and managed from a web page. Webmail accounts from major providers are completely free and independent, not tied to whoever provides your broadband, mobile phone etc.

The fact that a Webmail account is independent means you never need to change it. You can keep using the same account for many years to come.

Webmail is also great because you can check it from just about anywhere – an Internet café, a friend's computer, even a mobile phone.

There are four major providers of Webmail accounts, with many millions of users of each:

● **Mac email** is for Mac users and is very good. (You can also get an email account from Apple that ends in **@me.com**. This seems awfully precious to, well, 'me'.)

If you own a Mac, a .mac account is a great idea. However, if you think you may switch to a Windows machine someday, you may want to consider one of the others.

● **Hotmail** was the first Webmail provider and continued to grow fast after it was acquired by Microsoft some years ago. Microsoft has played around with the service, recently renaming it Windows Live Hotmail, without improving it much. In my opinion, Hotmail has fallen behind other top competitors, but remains a popular option nonetheless.

● **Yahoo Mail** is offered by the Yahoo! website, which was the first highly popular search engine and a significant provider of email, online message boards and other services. Yahoo Mail was an early leader and continues to be regularly improved.

It does have lots of big ads displayed in the free version. The biggest downside of Yahoo Mail is that, unless you sign up for the paid edition, at about £10 a year, you can't use it with Outlook or Apple Mail, as I recommend below.

Reproduced with permission of Yahoo! Inc. © 2009 Yahoo! Inc. YAHOO!, the YAHOO! logo and FLICKR and the FLICKR logo are registered trademarks of Yahoo! Inc

Figure 11.1

- **Google Mail** is my personal favourite, despite one major problem which I'll describe in a moment. It's free, free, free! You'll never have any reason to need to pay for it. (It does carry ads, but they're small, unobtrusive text-only ads.) Google Mail is fast, has almost unlimited storage capacity and works very well with Outlook and Apple Mail, as well as many other email packages.

  You can access your existing Google Mail emails and craft replies when you're not online, then send them once you have a connection. You can even use Google Mail to receive and reply to emails sent to your other accounts without ever visiting them, making it a sort of one-stop shop for all your email.

With all that good news, what's the major problem with Google Mail that I mentioned?

Google Mail bunches the messages you send and people's replies into 'conversations'. To clarify, it means that the original message, the reply, the reply to the reply, etc. are all arranged together into one group. It can therefore be quite hard to find a specific message, or to see the notification of a new message, within the back and forth of the conversation. This irritates some users; others like it.

If you really dislike Google Mail's conversations, Yahoo Mail may be the better choice. Take a look at the screenshots shown here to see which feels more comfortable for you. Consider visiting the websites and looking online at reviews. You may even want to sign up for both and try them – being sure not to give out your email address to friends and family until you're sure which one you want to use, of course.

You can work around Google Mail's conversations using the technique I describe below, using Microsoft Outlook or Apple Mail on your laptop as the permanent home for your email. Then you only have to deal with conversations when you're using Google Mail through a web interface; for instance, at an Internet café.

Reproduced from Google™ © 2009

Figure 11.2

Google Mail or Gmail?

Ever forget to pay a bill on time? Google made a similar mistake and it affects Google Mail users to this day.

In most of the world, Google's email service is called Gmail, a short, catchy, 'cool' name.

However, in the UK, the name Gmail was already registered to someone else. Google didn't check this properly and settle things before launching the service. As a result, the service is now called 'Google Mail' in the UK and Gmail everywhere else. You can often use the email address '**yourname@gmail.com**' as a kind of shortcut, but to avoid any possible problems, it's best to use the full name that applies to UK users: '**yourname@googlemail.com**'.

Using Webmail on your laptop

Laptops are great for email because they provide the best opportunity to use your own computer for email access most of the time. Webmail is perfect for enabling email access from a computer other than your own, or from a mobile phone.

What's the best way to use email on your laptop, though?

Millions of users have tried various ways of doing this and have come up with the answer I myself use every day. Run Microsoft Outlook on your laptop and use it to bring the email from your Webmail account, plus any other email accounts you have, into one convenient place.

If you have Microsoft Office then you have Outlook. Outlook includes:

- An excellent email program; many (including me) would say the best ever developed for Windows.
- A calendar for organising appointments.
- A Contacts area that serves as an address book.
- A Tasks list for keeping your to-do list handy.

It's hard to describe briefly just how great Outlook is. When it comes to computers, including laptops, Apple is often cited as a company that consistently gets all the little things right to create a really excellent experience overall. That's how I think of Outlook when it comes to personal information management software.

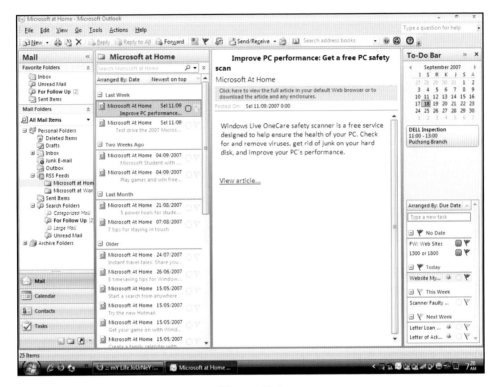

Figure 11.3

Part of the reason that I take my laptop with me, even when I could use another computer nearby instead, is to keep using my Outlook setup.

While Outlook has many features, its core function is email management. Here are the big pluses as I see them. Outlook:

● Lists emails one at a time or by conversation. (You can see emails one by one, even if they come from Google Mail, which will only display emails in conversations.)

- Allows you to sort emails by who sent the email, by whether it has an attachment, and other criteria, as well as by date.

- Makes it very easy to create folders into which you can sort your emails, without saving them to your hard disk. (The folders are reflected as 'labels' in Google Mail.)

- Has excellent integration with many other mail packages, including Google Mail.

Put simply, if you use Outlook with Google Mail, you get the best of both worlds. Outlook works as your daily email and personal information management program. Google Mail's web interface is your tool for when you're away from your laptop.

There are two ways to synchronise email among different programs: IMAP and POP3. If available, use the newer standard, IMAP. With POP3 it's all too easy for messages to appear on one system but not on another. Google Mail is the leader among Webmail programs in providing free IMAP support.

Outlook is also the best program for synchronising to a mobile phone. Because Outlook is so well established, the creators of other programs and of different hardware devices devote their best efforts to synchronising with it.

This includes Google. The Google Mail site has excellent and detailed instructions for synchronising Google Mail and Outlook. Look on the Google Mail site for instructions.

As soon as you decide on a Webmail provider and get your new account, move quickly to direct all your email to it. If you have other email accounts, even ones you don't use, go to them and reply to anyone who's used them (and from whom you still want to hear) giving your new email address. Look for any settings that let you automatically forward your email from that account to your new Webmail account. That way, even if you never use your old email again, you'll still ensure you catch any straggler correspondence from people who have not updated their contact details for you. After a while, you may want to consider deleting the old account, just to ensure no emails can still be sent there.

Using online search

The Web was invented in 1990 by a Brit, Tim Berners-Lee, working on a scientific project at the CERN laboratories in Switzerland. (He's since been knighted, and is now Sir Tim!) Berners-Lee has never tried to claim any kind of royalties from his invention, even during the crazy days of Internet startup companies in the late 1990s. Instead he writes, speaks, and travels to participate in continuing efforts to improve the Web.

Even in its early days, when there wasn't that much information online compared to today, searching the Web was quite a challenge. It still is today, but the tools are much better, and constantly improving.

There are three leading tools for searching the Web, or search engines as they are known. It is no coincidence they have been developed by the same people who provide the leading Webmail programs:

● Google Search is by far the leader. For many people, it is the only search engine they use. Such is Google's prominence, 'to Google' has even become a verb! You may well have heard people say that they will just 'Google it' to find information. I'll give a few tips and tricks for using Google Search here.

● Bing is Microsoft's new search engine. To the surprise of many Google fans, it's actually quite good, and even provides some answers that are better than Google's. Try a Bing search and see how you like it compared to Google.

● Yahoo Search was an early leader, but its popularity has dwindled comparatively in recent years. At the time of writing, rumour has it that Yahoo Search will disappear, replaced by Bing.

● Wikipedia is not a search engine but an online encyclopedia. Search Wikipedia for articles about a variety of subjects. A word of caution however. Wikipedia, as with all 'wiki' sites, allows users to create and edit content freely. While on the whole, Wikipedia is pretty accurate, it is advisable to verify important information elsewhere.

To use the leading search engine, Google Search, just visit Google at **www.google.co.uk**. (Most of the time, if you enter **www.google.com** from a computer in the UK, you'll be redirected to **www.google.co.uk** anyway.) Enter a term or terms related to what you're searching for. Results will appear onscreen;

you can scroll down or go to several pages of results to find exactly what you want.

The idea of hypertext – text with direct links to other text – was first popularised by Ted Nelson in the 1960s. There followed several decades of discussion, experimentation and early use before the Web exploded into widespread use in the 1990s.

Reproduced from Google™ © 2009

Figure 11.4

Here are some tips to help you get more out of Google Search:

- **Go national**. To search UK sites only, click the button, pages from the UK, before you search. This is great for finding stores and so on in the UK only, and for getting a British take on the news or some other topic.

- **Go global**. To get a truly global look, click the link, Go to **Google.com**, before searching. This ensures that there's no UK-based filtering or reordering of results.

- **Go local**. To find information locally, type in the name of a town, city or street along with the other search terms. You can also use **Yell.com** as an alternative to Google for business searches in a given area, or search from Google Maps, at **maps.google.com**.

Reproduced by permission of Yell Limited 2010. All rights reserved

Figure 11.5

- **Use the ads**. Many businesses use Google for advertisements for their goods and services. The ads are displayed to the side of, and sometimes above, the normal results. Ads can often be as good as the unpaid, 'organic' search results that Google serves up naturally.

Reproduced from Google™ © 2009

Figure 11.6

● **Use SafeSearch**. SafeSearch keeps much of the pornography and other junk that's out there on the Web out of your search results. When you first visit Google search, SafeSearch is set to the middle level, 'moderate' filtering. To tighten this up, especially if you have children using your computer, click the Preferences link from the main Google page. Change SafeSearch Filtering to strict filtering, the most restrictive. Then click Save Preferences to save the change.

● **Search wikis**. In addition to Wikipedia, there are several other 'wiki' sites with organised articles about different types of information. If you include the phrase 'wiki' in your search, these sites will come to the top. Don't forget: as mentioned previously, wikis are collaborative sites, created and edited by the users themselves, and so are open to human error and bias.

● **Try Bing**. When companies compete to provide the best products and services, ordinary people often benefit. Microsoft is trying hard to beat Google with its Bing search engine, especially by answering your query in the search results instead of requiring you click to different sites. Try your search on Bing and see if you learn something new.

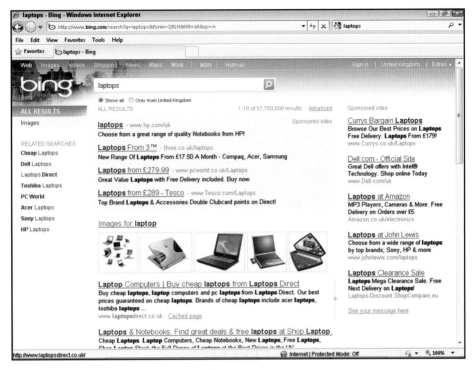

Figure 11.7

Finding videos, music and more online

You can find a lot of great music and videos online. Some of it isn't supposed to be there; people illegally copy songs, TV shows and even Hollywood movies and place them online. You don't want to be part of this; not only is it unfair to the copyright holders, such content often comes with viruses and other programs that damage your computer.

However, there's also a lot of great legal music and video content online. Here are a few sites you can visit for some of the very best – all legal and free:

● **YouTube**. You should visit YouTube, if only to try it. You may end up spending countless hours looking at silly videos, but it's more interesting than spending the same time looking at TV. Look up 'skateboarding dog' to find some of the more famous silly videos on YouTube. You can also upload your own videos to YouTube and share them, all free. Visit:

www.youtube.com

Some of the videos you find on YouTube may be unsuitable for any children who may be visiting you. Consider previewing the videos in a given area before searching YouTube with a child sitting next to you.

Reproduced with permission of Google™

Figure 11.8

● **Spotify**. Spotify is an excellent site for music played to you from your computer. You can find almost any album or song you like and play it. The free version includes an advert every few songs, but far fewer than on a typical radio station. The paid version is ad-free. Also, you're one up on your American friends: Spotify is not available in the States due to licensing restrictions, but it's perfectly legal in the UK and across Europe. Visit:

www.spotify.com

● **BBC iPlayer**. BBC iPlayer lets you watch the last week's BBC programs, including the extra digital channels that not all of us get. iPlayer is so popular it's been blamed for causing Internet bottlenecks in the UK all by itself. It's a great way to catch up on something you've missed. Like Spotify, it's not available in the US. (In iPlayer's case, nor anywhere else outside the UK.) Visit:

www.bbc.co.uk/iplayer/

● **Other 'iPlayers'**. Other UK TV channels have their own iPlayer-like sites, though usually with less content, due to licensing restrictions from program providers. For ITV, Channel 4 and Channel 5 respectively, visit:

www.itv.com/catchup

www.channel4.com/programmes/4od

demand.five.tv

There are a few other popular sites that may be of interest:

● **Flickr**. Flickr is the leading online photo management and sharing website. If you want to hook up a digital camera to your computer or upload your photos to share with others, Flickr is the most popular choice. Visit:

www.flickr.com

Reproduced with permission of Yahoo! Inc. © 2009 Yahoo! Inc. YAHOO!, the YAHOO! logo and FLICKR and the FLICKR logo are registered trademarks of Yahoo! Inc

Figure 11.9

● **Skype**. Skype allows you to make free calls from one computer to another and inexpensive calls to land lines both in the UK and internationally. (Calls to mobiles are cheaper than calling from a land line or mobile phone, but much more expensive than other Skype calls.) Visit:

www.skype.com

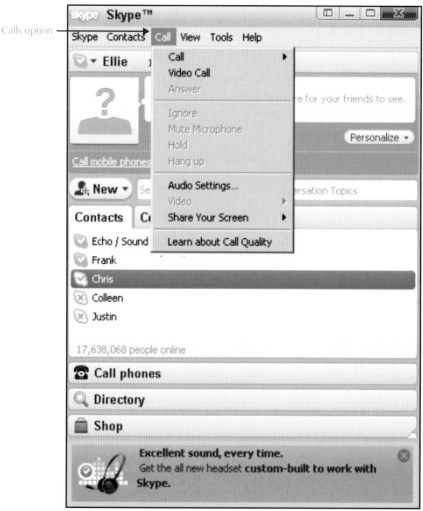

Reproduced from Skype Limited

Figure 11.10

● **iTunes**. It will come as no surprise to learn that downloading songs costs money. On iTunes, the current price per track is 79p. The advantage of a site such as iTunes is that you can usually buy just the particular tracks you want, rather than having to purchase the whole CD. Consequently, you can build up a sizeable library of songs at a moderate cost. If you later get a digital music player such as an iPod, you can easily put the songs you've purchased online onto the iPod or similar device as well. Visit:

www.apple.com/itunes

- **Blogger**. Blogs are simple websites that function much like a diary or journal; except this is a journal you intentionally want others to read. Blogs allow you to record your 'thoughts for the day', opinion about a news item or comments on last night's TV, along with photos, videos – pretty much anything. They can be a great way to keep people up to date with what you're doing or to share memories. Blogger is the simplest to use of the blogging sites. Find Blogger at:

www.blogger.com

- **Twitter**. Twitter is a popular online social networking and 'micro-blogging' service. Users send 'Tweets' (short messages of up 140 characters) to 'followers' (people signed up to follow the regular postings of one another). Twitter is often used to break news items also. For example, it was used to send the first photographs of the jet that landed in New York's Hudson River in 2009. Setting up and maintaining a Twitter account will undoubtedly increase your 'cool credentials' among your younger relatives! Go to:

www.twitter.com

Summary

- In the last 20 years, the Web has burgeoned to global, mainstream proportions.

- Email is the most important online application.

- A Webmail account is free and independent of services you may be paying for.

- Online searching is the gateway to finding what you need on the Web, and Google is the most popular online search engine.

- Videos and songs are now available online legally and are available to download.

Brain Training

There may be more than one correct answer to these questions.

1. What kind of email account does this book recommend?

a) A free email account from your broadband provider

b) An AOL account

c) A free Webmail account

d) A free email account from your mobile phone provider

2. Which personal organising software does this book recommend?

a) Lotus Notes

b) Microsoft Outlook

c) Google Apps

d) Palm Desktop

3. What's a good way to organise and access emails?

a) By date, as you receive them

b) Collected into conversations

c) By sender

d) In folders

4. What is the nationality of the Web's inventor?

a) British

b) Russian

c) French

d) American

5. What should you do with ads that show up in Google Search?

a) Ignore them

b) Use them when it makes sense to do so

c) Click on all of them

d) Report the advertisers to Ofcom

Answers

Q1 – c   **Q2** – b   **Q3** – a, b, c and d   **Q4** – a

Q5 – b

Preventing problems

Equipment needed: A laptop with wireless Internet access (see Chapter 9).

Skills needed: some knowledge of the keyboard, mouse and operating system to try further options and change more settings to suit your preference (see Chapters 7–9).

The Hippocratic Oath for doctors begins with the words: 'First, do no harm'.

Laptops are wonderful tools that can enrich our lives in many ways. Unfortunately, their very convenience can mean they are often exposed to harm. The more obvious are the physical kinds: losing your laptop, having it stolen, and breaking it.

The more subtle types of problems have to do with the software and data stored on the system. Examples of this are: the system becoming corrupted by viruses or other problems; having our personal information stolen; losing data.

The good news is that there's a lot you can do to help yourself with minimum effort. The old saying that an ounce of prevention is worth a pound of cure was never truer than when it comes to taking care of your laptop – either its physical state, or the software and data stored on it.

Follow the steps in this chapter to help protect yourself, and reduce your potential exposure to these kinds of issues.

Preventing loss or theft

Having your laptop lost or stolen is one of the most infuriating things that can happen. It's really several disasters at once: not only do you lose a valuable piece of equipment, you also lose your data (unless it's backed up separately) and all the time and effort you put into setting things up to your liking. There's also the general sense of anger and frustration that go with losing something of value or, worse, having someone steal from you.

Laptops are a prime target for thieves. Sadly, there are idiots out there who have no scruples when it comes to appropriating other people's goods for cash. The most prominent and obvious targets are probably wallets and purses, followed by watches and jewellery, car stereos; and of course, laptops.

Once my wife had her laptop stolen from our home, then fought off the burglar to get it back. You don't want to have to go through anything like that!

Luckily, avoiding problems is fairly easy with a little forethought. Here are some of the most important steps you can take to keep your laptop safe and secure.

In your home

The majority of laptops are kept at home most of the time. Unfortunately, that doesn't mean they are immune to theft.

No one can steal your laptop from your home if they don't know about it. Resist the urge to tell a lot of people about your new laptop. Keep the news among close friends and family.

Keep your laptop out of direct view from ground floor windows, and don't open it up where it's easily viewed even from windows on other floors. (Which is what the police told my wife and me after our misadventure.) Consider closing curtains or blinds when you're out of the house, even just for a bit, to keep thieves from 'taking inventory' through your windows and planning a burglary.

Just as showy items like jewellery and so on will attract thieves, similarly, high profile logos will also catch their attention. Thieves know the Apple logo means more money, just like you and I do. Sony is another brand that thieves, unfortunately, know and covet.

Consider putting your laptop away when you have strangers in – builders, salespeople and so on. The person in question may not be a thief, but they can mention something about your possessions to someone who is. It's not that you specifically distrust any one person, it's just another way to avoid being vulnerable.

If you have a lot of people in and out for various reasons, or if you live in any kind of shared accommodation, consider getting a lock for your laptop to use even when it's at home. This might seem like overkill, but preventing problems in this way is much easier than dealing with the aftermath of a theft.

Figure 12.1

The police explained to my wife and I that many thieves are like children; they're impulsive and respond strongly to what they see. If they don't see it, they won't try to get it. Keep your laptop out of sight.

> Take advantage of your laptop's portability when buying a lock for it. Just take the laptop with you to the computer shop. Ask for help finding a lock and have the salesperson show you how the lock hooks to your laptop; try connecting and removing the lock right there in the shop so you know you are bringing home a solution, not a problem.

Out and about

Whenever you take your laptop out of the house, 'loss' and 'theft' are often intertwined. If you carried a packed lunch out of the house, and you turned your back on it for a minute, it would probably still be there when you turned around. With a laptop, this may not be so likely. If you lose track of your laptop, even briefly, the loss could quickly turn into a theft, although you may never know exactly when it went from one to the other.

It might be wise to invest in a laptop lock. For example, if you type in 'laptop lock' on the PC World website (see Figure 2.2) it shows you the options available.

When avoiding theft of something valuable, people often say 'don't let it out of your sight'. With a laptop, there are actually two parts to this. The first part is, don't let it out of your *grasp*.

Don't leave your laptop on a table in a coffee shop, for instance, while you go to the counter to order. It's all too easy for someone to jostle you in the queue while someone else uses that moment to grab your laptop and head out the door. To prevent this, you can take a lock along to secure your laptop if needed. For instance, if you're going to spend the day in the library using the laptop, this might be a good approach. Be sure that defeating the lock isn't just a matter of lifting a table leg to slip off a coil of metal.

The second part has to do with sight. The comic Steve Martin used to tell a joke about the martial arts movie, 'Crouching Tiger, Hidden Dragon'. He was disappointed not to see either of the animals in it, until he realised: "The tigers were *crouching* and the dragons were *hidden*".

Search box

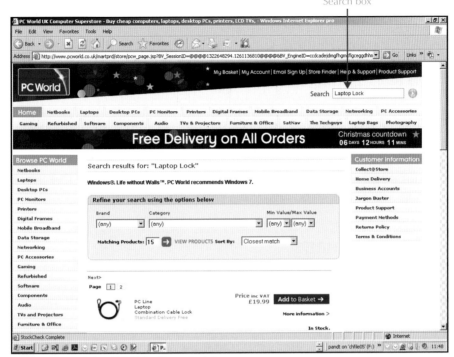

Reproduced by permission of © DSG Retail International plc

Figure 12.2

It's the same with your laptop when you take it out and about: keep it hidden. Put it in a sleeve to protect it from scratches and to keep that shiny metal out of the sight of potential thieves. Other than the sleeve, keep it in an ordinary bag, not a special laptop bag, and don't have any tech gear, such as a power plug, in view. Try not to have high-profile, highly desirable logos such as Apple, HP, or Sony showing.

Think twice before you take your laptop out of the bag to use it. Are you in a safe place surrounded by people who appear to be trustworthy? Would you feel safe taking out your wallet and counting the money in it in front of them? If so, you're probably OK using your laptop. If in doubt, read a newspaper instead.

I may be painting a fairly alarming picture, but my goal is to increase your awareness, not to frighten you. We all think twice before going into certain areas or going out alone at night. With a laptop, it's simply a matter of being that extra bit more careful. Once this becomes a habit, you won't be worried, just prudent.

Travelling

If you've flown on an airplane in the last few years, you've no doubt noticed your fellow travellers taking laptops out of their carry-on bags to be inspected in the security check. Now that you have a laptop, you will need to join them.

In most countries, it may also be fairly safe to travel with your laptop packed in a suitcase that's checked-in, as long as it doesn't obviously show from outside. You can't lock a suitcase these days; the authorities need to be able to get in and check it for illegal materials. However, it's strongly recommended that you keep your laptop with you as hand luggage.

Preventing damage

Loss, theft and damage are interrelated. They can all demonstrate how the positive attributes of a laptop – its portability, flexibility and sheer usefulness – can become negatives.

You take your laptop to a coffee house and spill coffee on it. You take it into the kitchen table and it falls off onto the hard floor. You plug it in at the library and someone trips on the power cord, sending the laptop, and possibly themselves, flying. With a little forethought, you can avoid all these issues.

Ten steps to protect your laptop

There are a few specific thoughts to keep in mind when it comes to protecting your laptop from damage and breakage:

1. **Keep drinks away**. If you make a habit of having a drink near your laptop, you'll probably spill it into the laptop at some point. Keep it well away.

2. **Tipping distance**. If you must have a drink while you work on your laptop, keep cups, cans and bottles 'falling distance' away from the laptop. That means, if they tip over, they still won't quite spill into it. Having the drink arm's length away from you and a bit behind the laptop is a good solution.

3. **Think twice about the power cord**. Then think again. Laptop power cords are an accident waiting to happen. Run on battery if you feel there may be a risk.

4. **Centre the laptop**. It's much easier for your laptop to fall off the edge of a table than the middle. Keep it at least a hand's length from any edge of the work surface.

5. **Keep the laptop closed**. When you're not using the laptop, close it. This prevents all sorts of interesting screen breakage possibilities and reduces the potential for snapping the screen off from the base. It also reduces the 'eye candy' appeal to potential thieves.

6. **Don't use it on a pillow or blanket**. Your laptop depends on a small but crucial amount of airflow along the base to keep cool. Resting it on a pillow, cushion or blanket cuts off the airflow and brings dust right up against the vents.

7. **Keep it off the floor**. It's easy to step or trip on a laptop once it's there, or even to put heavy things on it. Keep your laptop off the floor, full stop.

8. **Check your screen type**. Some laptop screens are pretty resistant to scratches and cracking; others are quite delicate. You can get a feel for this by rubbing the back of your finger across it. My current laptop's screen has a plastic-like feel to it that seems to indicate that it's pretty resistant to scratches and cracking.

9. **Be careful with connectors**. We've all jammed a resistant plug into a socket, but think twice before doing this on your computer. They are not that robust and prone to damage should you let frustration get the better of you by using excessive force.

10. **Handle with care**. Laptops are so easy to deal with you can find yourself taking yours for granted. Protect your laptop, and yourself, by treating it like the delicate thing it is. Put it in hibernate mode before moving it. Get both feet under you and square your body before lifting it. Check that your path is clear, especially underfoot, before carrying it across the room. Don't carry an open laptop up or down stairs. Make sure the area around your laptop is clear before opening it.

You can probably come up with your own additional steps that apply specifically to the way you use your laptop. They all represent an extra level of care to help prevent those 'Oh no!' moments.

A near miss is as good as a mile?

In studying safety, companies that really focus on preventing accidents have learned to pay attention to 'near misses' – accidents that almost happen. If you prevent near misses, you of course prevent actual accidents as well.

When you almost spill a drink on the keyboard, almost trip on a cord, or almost drop your laptop, you've just had a valuable learning experience.

What if you do spill something into your laptop?

If you spill water or a drink into your laptop, follow these three simple steps:

1. **Turn the power off at the wall**. Naturally, you don't want liquid contacting 'live' circuits inside the laptop, or they will short. But you don't want to touch the laptop while that's happening, or *you* may short! So cut off the power by disconnecting at the wall socket right away. It keeps you out of danger while giving you the best chance to salvage your laptop. Then unplug the computer and remove the battery (if it's removable) to prevent power of any kind flowing through the laptop. Check that the battery, its connectors and the mains power connector aren't wet; if they are, head to the repair shop (step 3).

2. **Assess the damage**. With the computer unplugged and the battery removed, turn the computer upside down and sideways and shake it gently. If any water comes out, don't turn it on; go straight to step 3. If everything's quite dry, and you feel sure the liquid stayed on the surface, consider powering the computer up again on battery power.

If things look bad, a good repair shop will remove your hard disk and try powering your laptop up with a different one. This ensures that your hard disk data can be saved even if the laptop is a loss.

3. **Head to the repair shop**. When in doubt, take your laptop to a shop. If possible, go to the shop you bought it at, as they have a stake in seeing that you go away happy. Consider asking to watch the initial check so you can learn from what happened. The repair shop can open your laptop, check for water penetration, and can clean and dry off any liquid before supplying power.

With an average, new laptop costing £300–£400, and parts adding to the cost, it doesn't take many hours of repairs at around £50 an hour to make you wonder – should I just get a new laptop?

The experts' rule of thumb is that you should consider buying a new product if fixing the old one would cost more than 30–40% of the price of a new one. So get an estimate up front. If the bill will be more than £100 or so, seriously consider replacing, rather than repairing, your laptop.

Preventing freezes and slowdowns

One of the most frustrating aspects of using a laptop is the way it may seem to slow down over time as you use it. There are several potential causes for this.

- **Changes in expectations**. The first cause of a 'slowdown' is simply changes in your expectations. As you get more accustomed to using your computer, you are more focused on your task than on the steps to do it, and the computer seems frustratingly slow. Cursing this kind of 'slowdown' is like cursing traffic on the roads; comforting, perhaps, but not actually helpful.

- **Accumulation of programs**. As you add programs to your system, each can modify the system software, adding code that runs at startup and takes up memory, even when it's not running. Normal usage of your laptop, such as adding a new digital camera or mobile phone, updating a Web browser or Flash multimedia software causes programs to accumulate.

- **Disk fragmentation**. As you use your computer, program and data files can become split across the hard disk in unhelpful ways, and this negatively impacts on speed. Run the built-in disk defragmentation utility every month or two to reverse this. On Windows, it's in the System Tools folder: Start ➪ All Programs ➪ Accessories ➪ System Tools ➪ Disk Defragmentation. In Windows 7 you can simply click the Start button and type 'defrag' to find the program. Allow for around an hour for the program to run while you're not using the computer.

- **Virus infestations**. It's easy for your computer to suffer from virus infestations that gradually slow it down. While anti-virus programs help, they don't prevent all problems. The only certain solution is to restore your system from the system disk, after backing up your data.

● **Attempts to fix it**. Many major problems are caused whilst trying to fix minor problems. I recently threw away most of my stored documents by accident (a big problem) while trying to clear up all the junk on my desktop (a small problem).

Many 'fix-it' programs are themselves viruses or programs for stealing data and so on. Only use trusted, name-brand 'fix-it' programs or get help from a repair shop.

When you experience a system slow-down, first try defragmenting your hard disk, as described above. Then there are two major options you can consider:

1. Backing up your data, then re-installing the operating system, applications and data.

2. Taking your computer to a shop where they'll use one or more clean-up tools and, if needed, they can also re-install the operating system, applications and data for you.

For most of us, taking the computer to a reputable shop is the safest and easiest option.

Explaining how to carry out a backup and re-installation would probably require a book in itself. Consider finding a friend or family member experienced in these things, who would be willing to spend an afternoon going through the process with you. If possible, back up your data before the friend arrives. Once they arrive to help, get them to do an additional back up. This provides two chances to save your vital information.

Preventing loss of data

Regularly backing up your data is very important, yet, ironically, the attempt itself can sometimes cause people to lose data.

Unlike disk defragmentation (described above), there's no one tool you can run that produces a good, reliable backup with no further work on your part. Instead there are many ways to back up data, system settings and so on, each of which solves some, but not all, of the problem.

In this section I'll concentrate on backing up your data. I've learned a few approaches over the years that can help.

- **Using email for storage**. Every week, email important files to yourself. You can be casual about this and just email files you've worked on recently. Or you can be more systematic and email whole folders full of files by date or type.

  Working on books, I depend on this approach quite a bit. My photos are on my mobile phone and my wife's computer. My chapters and graphics images are regularly sent to editors as I submit my work. Although I wouldn't want to bother my editors to recover them, the point is that the files are all out there as email attachments, which I can easily find and retrieve.

- **Using a USB drive (memory stick)**. You may be able to use one or two USB drives for backup. You simply plug in the USB drive, then drag folders from your Documents folder onto the USB drive. You may want to use separate

Reproduced with permission of Yahoo! Inc. © 2009 Yahoo! Inc. YAHOO!, the YAHOO! logo and FLICKR and the FLICKR logo are registered trademarks of Yahoo! Inc

Figure 12.3

USB drives for photos and other documents. You may also want to use a service like Flickr, which not only publishes your photos for others to see but provides a kind of backup at the same time.

● **Using an online or 'in-house' backup service**. There are online services, as well as devices you can buy for your home, that invite you to back up your files with them. These can be quite useful and make recovery easy. I'd tend to favour the online option; fire and flood are two of the biggest dangers to your laptop's data over time, and either of them might wipe out an in-house backup device right along with your laptop.

● **Working in 'the cloud'**. I haven't mentioned this option much in this book, but some brave souls – even companies – are using online applications and data storage for their routine work. Your actual computer becomes a kind of temporary storage device for your work and parts of your programs, which actually 'live' online. My habit of depending on emailed files, or using Flickr for photos, is a 'light' form of this; working in the cloud all the time should mean that your data is always available and never at risk of being lost.

In addition to actually losing data, there's the problem of losing track of data. That is, not being able to find the file you created three weeks ago with your notes from talking to your solicitor, or something equally important.

Apple has several utilities for backup and file finding on the Mac. Microsoft has actually *weakened* the file finder it used to have on earlier versions of Windows. You used to be able to, for instance, specify what kind of file to search for. Microsoft has apparently decided we're all too dim to deal with this kind of complexity and removed the option from searches.

I'm being harsh, though. The kind of unrestricted search Microsoft is now offering is closer to the kind of search people are accustomed to with Google and even Microsoft's own Bing search engine, so it's probably a positive move.

Microsoft has also made the search function easier to find and use. Let's say I want to find a file I'd written, which mentions Google Voice, (a new service from Google). I'd follow these steps to find it:

1. Click the Start button.

    The Start menu appears.

2. Click the Search box.

    The Search box is just above the Start button.

Getting Started ▶

Windows Media Center

Calculator

Sticky Notes

Snipping Tool

Paint

Magnifier

Solitaire

▶ All Programs

Search programs and files 🔍

Chris

Documents

Pictures

Music

Games

Computer

Control Panel

Devices and Printers

Default Programs

Help and Support

Shut down ▷

Search box

Figure 12.4

3. Type the term you're searching for. I'm looking for Google Voice. I want the two words as one term, so I enter them in quotes: 'google voice'. (Capitalisation doesn't matter in most searches.)

As you type, a window above the search box fills with the names of files that contain your search term.

The Shut down button remains visible as you proceed with the search and view the results. Be careful not to click it accidentally.

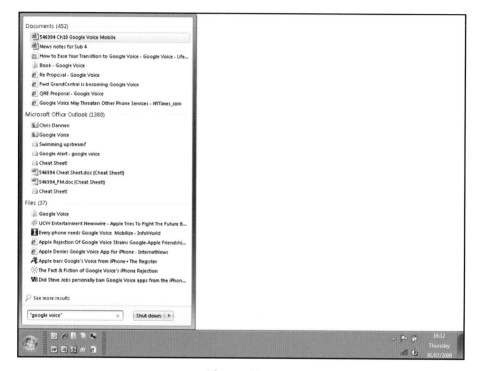

Figure 12.5

4. Click the link, See more results.

   A window opens with your search results. It includes files with the words you searched for in the file name or within the file itself.

5. Click the maximise button in the upper right of the window to expand it.

   Searching is easier the more you can see, and maximising the window helps.

6. Click the Change your view button in the upper right area of the window to see the different views you can have on the files listed.

   Options appear: extra large icons, large icons, medium icons, small icons, list, details, tiles and content.

You can change the preview area from visible to hidden and back by using the Preview Pane button in the upper right corner.

7. Click Details.

   The contents of the window appear with 'details' such as the file size and the folder name.

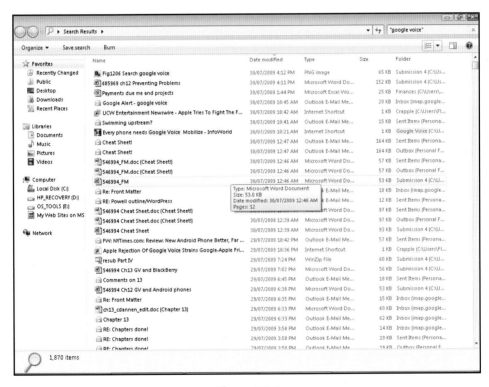

Figure 12.6

8. Click the column header, Date modified.

   The column contents sort by the date each file was last changed, with the newest files near the top. (The small triangle next to the words, Date modified, points down.)

9. Click the column header, Date modified, again.

The sorting is reversed: the column contents sort by the date each file was last changed, with the oldest files now near the top. (The small triangle next to the words, Date modified, points up.)

10. Continue trying different ways to view and sort to become familiar with them.

Larger icons are great for previewing images and formatted documents; the Details view is good when you know something about the file such as its approximate modification date, size or type.

The techniques you use in searching for a file are valuable in Internet searching and in other kinds of searches on your computer, such as looking for a file in a specific folder.

A mistake that even experienced users make concerns receiving a document, such as a Word document, as an email attachment. The common response is to click on the file to open it, then immediately start editing it. The trouble is, if you then click save, the file is saved, but in a very low-level folder in a temporary storage area. It can be hard or even impossible to find the file again. The search techniques described above may be the only hope.

A final thought

A laptop is both the easiest and the most challenging type of computer to use. Most of the time, it's a 'win-win' situation – you get all the power you might expect from a desktop computer combined with the convenience of a device that you can take anywhere with you.

With a little care, you can keep your costs moderate while avoiding the potential pitfalls of mobility. Serving as a guide to this new world has been a challenge, and a lot of fun. I hope you've enjoyed reading this as much as I've enjoyed writing it, and that you refer to this book again and again.

Summary

- The very convenience of laptops can make them vulnerable.

- When your laptop is at home, keep it out of easy view of outsiders.

- Be careful when carrying your laptop and when setting a drink near it.

- Consider any dangers before deciding to take your laptop with you on a short or long trip.

- Back up your data regularly.

Brain Training

There may be more than one correct answer to these questions.

1. What steps should you take to prevent laptop theft?

a) When out and about, keep your laptop in reach

b) At home, keep your laptop out of sight of windows

c) Tell everyone you meet you have a laptop

d) Show off the brand of your laptop to impress people

2. What should you do if heading to a dodgy area or country?

a) Take your laptop anyway

b) Leave it at home if you can't be sure to protect it

c) Keep your laptop out of sight

d) Make sure there's wireless access

3. Where's a good place to set your laptop down?

a) On the floor

b) Toward the middle of a table

c) On the bar at the pub

d) On a chair

4. What should you do first if you spill something into your laptop?

a) Phone 999

b) Get a sponge

c) Call an online support service

d) Turn off the power at the wall

5. What's a good 'quick fix' for computer slowdowns?

a) Run a disk defragmentation program

b) Buy additional virus software

c) Back up your data

d) Send files to yourself via email to save them

Answers

Q1 – a and b   **Q2** – b and c   **Q3** – b   **Q4** – d

Q5 – a

PART IV
Glossary

He's just Googling "Repetitive Strain Injuries."...

©2009 Stephen Long

Glossary

Antivirus program A program that spots a virus on your computer or attached to an email and deals with it.

Application A computer program such as Word.

Backup Keeping copies of programs or work in a separate place, in case you lose the original or it gets corrupted.

Bandwidth A measure of the maximum amount of data that can be transferred over the Internet at any one time.

Bloatware Pre-installed, trial or basic versions of programs that you have to pay for to use fully.

Blog An online article, often presented in a 'diary' format, written by a 'blogger', who can be an individual, organisation or newspaper.

Bluetooth A short-range wireless system that enables devices to talk to each other. On your laptop, you might use Bluetooth to connect wirelessly to a headset, a mobile phone or a printer.

Boot To start up a computer.

Broadband A high-speed Internet connection that is always 'live'.

Browser Program to help you navigate the Internet (for example, Internet Explorer, Firefox and Safari).

Chipset The chips that keep the processor supplied with information and carry out its commands.

Control panel The area where you can configure the main functions of your computer.

Copy, and cut & paste Taking a cut or copy of a selected item (text or picture) and placing the copy somewhere else in the same document or another document or folder.

Cursor In a document, the cursor is the flashing icon indicating where you are and where your next keystroke will appear. When browsing web pages, the cursor enables you to point to and clink on commands and links.

Database A list of items of data stored in a computer system so it can be amended, searched or printed.

Desktop The screen as it is displayed when the computer is started up.

Desktop replacement A full-sized laptop with a screen size of 15" to 17" and weighing 6lb or more, mainly for use in the home, but can be carried around if need be.

Dongle A small piece of hardware that plugs into one of your laptop's USB ports and acts as the modem for the mobile broadband service.

Download The process of transferring files (pictures, documents or programs) from the Web to your machine's hard drive.

Drag and drop Selecting a file and dragging it to another position, such as a different folder.

Driver Software that enables a computer to work with an external device such as a digital camera, printer or scanner.

Dropdown menu A menu of options that appears when you click or hover the cursor over a heading.

Email Messages sent from one person to another over the Internet. Email addresses always include the @ symbol.

External monitor connection (or VGA connector) Allows you to hook up an external monitor to your laptop so you can use it instead of your laptop's built-in screen.

File extensions Three letters after a full stop at the end of every file name, which tell the computer what program to use to open the file (for example, .doc, .xls, .pdf, .jpg).

Files and folders The two main elements used to store computer documents.

Footprint The amount of space a laptop takes up on a desk.

Function keys Programmable keys numbered F1 to F13.

Hard disk/hard drive The main storage space of your computer. The higher the capacity of your hard disk, the more it can store. A 250GB hard drive should be enough for most users.

Hardware Any physical piece of computer equipment, such as a computer, keyboard or printer.

Hotmail A web-based email service owned by Microsoft.

Hotspot An area, for example in a cafe, airport or hotel, where Wi-Fi-enabled laptops or smartphones can connect to the Internet.

Icon Small symbol used to represent a file, folder, program, document or option.

ISP Internet Service Provider. The company that provides you with access to the Internet.

LCD panel and graphics The big, bright, beautiful screens that laptops are famous for.

Mac Apple Macintosh computer.

Megabits The maximum speed of your Internet connection is given in megabits per second (Mbps).

Memory *See RAM.*

Memory card reader Digital cameras, mobile phones, and other consumer electronics devices sold today use small, removable memory cards to store data. A memory card reader on your laptop allows you to read and transfer data from memory cards.

Memory stick or flash drive A small removable, rewritable device for storing data. Used in much the same way as floppy discs were once used.

Microblogging Blogging by 'tweeting' on Twitter, which limits the number of words you can use.

Microprocessor or CPU (Central Processing Unit) The brains of a computer. The two major manufacturers today are Intel and AMD.

Monitor The computer screen.

Netbook A laptop with a screen smaller than 10" and weighing about 2lb.

Network General term for a series of computers linked together wirelessly or with cables.

Notebook A laptop with screen size of 12" to 14" and weighing about 3-5lb.

Offline Not connected to the Internet.

Online Connected to the Internet.

Operating system The software that runs your computer and its programs. Windows is an operating system.

PC Personal computer.

Ports Sockets in a computer, into which external devices are plugged.

RAM Random Access Memory. This is the fast memory that the microprocessor uses to make things happen on your computer. Two gigabytes (2GB) of RAM is enough for most routine work. If a laptop has more than 2GB of RAM, it's a nice bonus.

Screenshot A digital 'photograph' taken by the computer to record what's displayed on the monitor or another device.

Scroll If a web page is too big to fit on the computer screen, you read it by 'scrolling' up and down.

Search engine A computer program that enables you to search for things on the Web. The three leading search engines are Google Search, Bing and Yahoo!

Skype A software application that allows users to communicate by text or voice over the Internet.

Sleep mode Turns off your monitor and stops the hard disk and internal components from running, when you're not using it.

Software Computer programs.

Spreadsheet A computer application similar to an accounting worksheet, which allows you to enter figures, make calculations and produce tables and graphs.

Taskbar (or Dock) The strip at the bottom of the screen, used to monitor and launch applications.

Trackpad A rectangle on your laptop's keyboard used instead of a mouse, for moving the cursor around. Laptops are typically equipped with a trackpad.

USB Universal Serial Bus. A device that allows you to connect a device such as a camera, printer, external mouse, memory stick or printer to your computer.

Virus A malicious program that can harm your computer, spread through programs from disks or the Internet.

Webcam A small camera attached to a computer.

Wi-Fi An interface that enables devices such as computers and mobile phones to connect to the Internet when they are within range.

Windows 7 The latest edition of the Windows operating system.

Word Microsoft's word processing application.

WWW Word Wide Web

Index

M

Mac, 136
  buying, 50
  Mac email, 217
  MacOS and included software, 41
  vs. PC, choice of, 16–18
  Windows laptop, comparing, 57–59
management, power, 154–155
  and Mac, 155–156
  Windows 7, 154–155
medium-sized widescreen, 3
memory card reader, 36
memory stick trick, 183
metal versus plastic casing, 22–23
microprocessor, 38
Microsoft Office, 41
Microsoft PowerPoint, 203
miniaturisation of batteries, 17
mobile broadband, 69, 72–74, 170,
    181–182
  Contract, 182
  Pay As You Go, 182
'Moore's Law', 40
mouse test, 94–96
multimedia settings, 161
music, finding online, 227–231
  BBC iPlayer, 228
  Flickr, 229
  iPlayer, 229
  Spotify, 228

N

netbooks, 29
  size, 14
network connector, 36
network icon in notifications, 171
notebooks, 29
Notepad, 191
notifications area, changing, 133–135
numeric keypad control, 33

O

old beliefs, challenging, 6–7
online, activities, 213–231
  backup service, 246
  best email account, 215–219
  email, 214–222
  learning, 5–6
  online access, working without,
    184–185
  Webmail, 220–222
online search, using, 223–227, *see also*
    Google Search
  BBC iPlayer, 228
  Blogger, 231
  Flickr, 229
  iTunes, 230–231
  music, 227–231
  Skype, 229–230
  Spotify, 228
  Twitter, 231
  videos, 227–231
  YouTube, 227–228
online shopping, 48–50
Outlook, 222

P

package deal, 76–79
Page up/Page down and arrow keys
    control, 33
Paint, 191
parts of laptop, 28–29
  invisible, 37–38
payment methods, 56–57
PC World (www.pcworld.co.uk), 49
PCI Express, 161
performance of laptop, 39
portability, 3–4, 8
power buttons, 161
power connector, 35
power cord, 164

R

S

T

Y

Older and Wiser
Technology
Made Easy

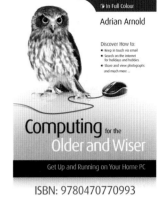

🌀 In Full Colour

Adrian Arnold

Discover How to:
- Keep in touch via email
- Search on the internet for holidays and hobbies
- Share and view photographs and much more ...

Computing for the
Older and Wiser

Get Up and Running on Your Home PC

ISBN: 9780470770993

THE THIRD AGE TRUST
U 3 A
THE UNIVERSITY OF THE THIRD AGE

Discover How to:
- Create, save and find documents
- Set up and use an email account
- Search the internet for news, shopping and travel
- Use your computer to view and share photos

Adrian Arnold
Computing with Windows 7
for the **Older and Wiser**

Get Up and Running on Your Home PC

ISBN: 9780470687031

THE THIRD AGE TRUST
U 3 A
THE UNIVERSITY OF THE THIRD AGE

Discover How to:
- Make the most of your holiday photos
- Save money online
- Keep in touch with family & friends
- Stay safe on the web

Adrian Arnold
The Internet for the
Older and Wiser

Get Up and Running Safely on the Web

ISBN: 9780470748398

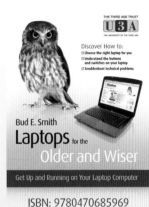

THE THIRD AGE TRUST
U 3 A
THE UNIVERSITY OF THE THIRD AGE

Discover How to:
- Choose the right laptop for you
- Understand the buttons and switches on your laptop
- Troubleshoot technical problems

Bud E. Smith
Laptops for the
Older and Wiser

Get Up and Running on Your Laptop Computer

ISBN: 9780470685969

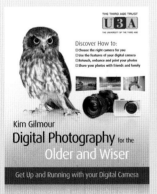

THE THIRD AGE TRUST
U 3 A
THE UNIVERSITY OF THE THIRD AGE

Discover How to:
- Choose the right camera for you
- Use the features of your digital camera
- Retouch, enhance and print your photos
- Share your photos with friends and family

Kim Gilmour
Digital Photography for the
Older and Wiser

Get Up and Running with your Digital Camera

ISBN: 9780470687024

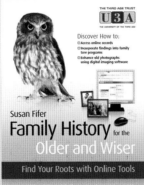

THE THIRD AGE TRUST
U 3 A
THE UNIVERSITY OF THE THIRD AGE

Discover How to:
- Access online records
- Incorporate findings into family tree programs
- Enhance old photographs using digital imaging software

Susan Fifer
Family History for the
Older and Wiser

Find Your Roots with Online Tools

ISBN: 9780470686126

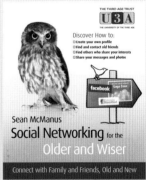

THE THIRD AGE TRUST
U 3 A
THE UNIVERSITY OF THE THIRD AGE

Discover How to:
- Create your own profile
- Find and contact old friends
- Find others who share your interests
- Share your messages and photos

Sean McManus
Social Networking for the
Older and Wiser

Connect with Family and Friends, Old and New

ISBN: 9780470686409

Available from your local bookshop or from
www.pcwisdom.co.uk

WILEY
Now you know.
wiley.com

12770